So many devotional books for teenagers fall prey to one or ~~more~~ missteps: they talk about the Bible but don't get young peop~~le~~; talk down to teenagers; or they try too hard to be cool (which just comes off as lame). *Experience the Gospel of Mark*, thankfully, avoids all these problematic approaches. It's straightforward, engaging, conversational, and invitational. And I *love* that *The Message* passages for each day are embedded in the text, which increases the likelihood that students will actually read them.

Mark Oestreicher, The Youth Cartel

As a family and student pastor, I am always looking for resources that challenge students and are Bible based. Here it is! *Experience the Gospel of Mark: 30 Days of Reading, Learning, and Living God's Word* is what I plan to give out to students who are hungry to dive into the Bible on their own. The structure and layout are easy for students to follow, and the experience and takeaway sections challenge the reader to not just have head knowledge but also apply what they are reading to their lives. *Yes. Yes! Yes!!* We need resources like this to help cultivate a rhythm of learning and a living out of our faith.

Christy Penley, students and family pastor at Pulpit Rock Church

Experience the Gospel of Mark gives students of the Bible a thirty-day immersion into the shortest of the four Gospels. Each reading offers readers the space to experience God through the text. The accessibility of *The Message* makes the experiential nature of this Bible study an inviting opportunity. *The Message* captures the sacred words of Mark's Gospel and communicates them in common, everyday language. The daily readings immerse readers in sizable passages from Mark and lead readers to reflect on how each passage can penetrate the heart and lead to spiritual formation.

Derek Vreeland, pastor and author of *Centering Jesus*

EXPERIENCE

THE GOSPEL OF

mark

30 Days of Reading, Learning, and Living God's Word

Andy Klenke

NavPress

A NavPress resource published in alliance
with Tyndale House Publishers

Experience the Gospel of Mark: 30 Days of Reading, Learning, and Living God's Word

Copyright © 2024 by Experience Scripture. All rights reserved.

A NavPress resource published in alliance with Tyndale House Publishers

Adapted from *Experience the Gospel of Mark* copyright © 2018 by Experience Scripture, xpscripture.com

The Team:
David Zimmerman, Publisher; Olivia Eldredge, Managing Editor; Jennifer L. Phelps, Designer; Sarah K. Johnson, Proofreading Coordinator

Some of the anecdotal illustrations in this book are true to life and are included with the permission of the persons involved. All other illustrations are composites of real situations, and any resemblance to people living or dead is purely coincidental.

For information about special discounts for bulk purchases, please contact Tyndale House Publishers at csresponse@tyndale.com, or call 1-855-277-9400.

ISBN 978-1-64158-907-9

Printed in China

30	29	28	27	26	25	24
7	6	5	4	3	2	1

contents

introduction

Who is Jesus? This question, as popular as it is today, was even more common two thousand years ago when Jesus walked the earth. Confusion and controversy followed this teacher from Bethlehem as He performed amazing miracles and spoke with confident authority. And while much of Jesus' teaching referenced familiar Old Testament passages and themes, He often drew new, and even uncomfortable, conclusions. The Gospel of Mark records the events of Jesus' life, prompting future readers to ask the same question the crowds asked during ancient times: *Who is Jesus?*

Here are some key overarching details to help you understand Mark's Gospel.

Author. Mark. Mark was known to be Peter's (Jesus' disciple's) trusted assistant.

Purpose. Mark provides a brief account of Jesus' time on earth. He writes about Jesus' ministry, healings, teaching, death, and resurrection. He writes to show that Jesus is the Son of God and Savior of the world!

Style. Fast-paced and action-packed. Mark rarely provides details or descriptive language—he gets right to the point!

Key verse. "That is what the Son of Man has done: He came to serve, not to be served—and then to give away his life in exchange for many who are held hostage." Mark 10:45

Themes.

- *The cost of discipleship*: Mark shows that while following Jesus may be costly, it is worth it.
- *Upside down*: Mark records Jesus' new, countercultural value system to mankind.
- *Son of God*: Mark's portrayal of Jesus leaves no doubt that He is indeed the Son of God.
- *Heart over rules*: Mark emphasizes that Jesus' ultimate concern is the condition of our hearts.
- *Love and compassion*: Mark highlights Jesus' love and compassion for the world through His miracles, teachings, and sacrifice.

Major characters.

- *Jesus*: The controversial Jewish leader who claimed to be the Son of God.
- *Pharisees*: Religious leaders who were experts in the Old Testament law. Pharisees had a reputation for prioritizing rules over a genuine relationship with God.
- *The disciples*: A group of twelve men whom Jesus chose to be His first followers. While they often misunderstood Jesus' words and actions, Jesus used this faithful group to advance His mission in incredible ways!

Terms to know.

- *Miracles*: Signs that show Jesus' power.
- *Parables*: Stories from everyday life that explain complicated truths.
- *The gospel*: The Good News of salvation, offered through Jesus' life, death, and resurrection.

how to get the most out of this book

This book, divided into thirty days of reading, learning, and living, is designed to help you experience Scripture. Use these step-by-step instructions to help understand how you can best use this tool.

Know before You Go

This section explains the background information you need in order to understand the day's Scripture. In other words, it gives some ideas for you to know before you go and read.

Read the Passage

The Scripture for the day's experience will be printed using *The Message* version of the Bible. Do not skip this reading! This is the most important step in your experience.

After the Passage

This section explores the messages, themes, or confusing parts in the day's Scripture. It is not meant to be the answer key, since we will not address every question or issue that you may have after reading the passage. The point is to introduce you to Scripture and help you understand the main idea, or bottom line, for each day.

The Bottom Line

This short statement distills the passage into a core concept for you to continue to reflect on.

Experience

This section creates space for you to process or experience each day's Scripture. The questions are meant to engage different parts of your mind, so each day's experience will vary in style. We want you to go beyond simply reading Mark. We want you to experience its truth for yourself. Take time to respond to the questions provided and be honest with yourself as you experience Scripture. Do not feel boxed in by the questions! Use this space to explore what God is teaching you.

Takeaway and Pray

This section prompts you to choose one personal application. Consider the ideas you have processed and commit to one as your main takeaway. Then focus your daily prayer on one specific request, confession, and/or praise. Naming this one specific prayer allows you to reflect on God's power and possible answer to prayer as time passes.

WE ARE EXCITED FOR
YOU TO EXPERIENCE THE
GOSPEL OF MARK OVER
THE NEXT THIRTY DAYS!

prepare
& point

Mark 1:1-15

Know before You Go

Mark explains how John the Baptist prepares people for Jesus' ministry on earth.

Read the Passage

1:1-3The good news of Jesus Christ—the Message!—begins here, following to the letter the scroll of the prophet Isaiah.

> Watch closely: I'm sending my preacher ahead of you;
> He'll make the road smooth for you.
> Thunder in the desert!
> Prepare for God's arrival!
> Make the road smooth and straight!

4-6John the Baptizer appeared in the wild, preaching a baptism of life-change that leads to forgiveness of sins. People thronged to him from Judea and Jerusalem and, as they confessed their sins, were baptized by him in the Jordan River into a changed life. John wore a camel-hair habit, tied at the waist with a leather belt. He ate locusts and wild field honey.

[7-8]As he preached he said, "The real action comes next: The star in this drama, to whom I'm a mere stagehand, will change your life. I'm baptizing you here in the river, turning your old life in for a kingdom life. His baptism—a holy baptism by the Holy Spirit—will change you from the inside out."

[9-11]At this time, Jesus came from Nazareth in Galilee and was baptized by John in the Jordan. The moment he came out of the water, he saw the sky split open and God's Spirit, looking like a dove, come down on him. Along with the Spirit, a voice: "You are my Son, chosen and marked by my love, pride of my life."

[12-13]At once, this same Spirit pushed Jesus out into the wild. For forty wilderness days and nights he was tested by Satan. Wild animals were his companions, and angels took care of him.

[14-15]After John was arrested, Jesus went to Galilee preaching the Message of God: "Time's up! God's kingdom is here. Change your life and believe the Message."

After the Passage

The Gospel of Mark introduces us to Jesus' ministry; however, it begins with a reference to the Old Testament (Mark 1:2-3 is quoting Malachi 3:1 and Isaiah 40:3). Even though we often talk about the Bible as two different parts—the Old Testament and the New Testament—they are actually two parts of the same story. When we see Old Testament verses quoted in the New Testament (like Mark 1:2-3), they are a reminder that Jesus' life continues the story of God in the Old Testament.

Mark 1:1-3 also shows us that John the Baptist's calling is significant because the Old Testament mentions it is going to happen hundreds of years before John the Baptist is even born. So try not to be fooled by his unique clothes and peculiar diet (Mark 1:6): He is actually an incredibly important person in the story of Jesus. John the Baptist is chosen by God to pave the way for Jesus and prepare people for the Good News they are about to hear (Mark 1:4-5). He is not some crazy guy walking around preaching a random sermon—he is specifically called by God to tell people about Jesus!

John's entire life purpose is to make sure that when Jesus arrives, people's hearts are ready to receive His message. Although John gains popularity and fame, he continues to use his platform to point others to Jesus. Think of how different this approach is from that of most celebrities! Typically, the more famous people get, the more they talk about themselves. John the Baptist does the exact opposite: He points others to Jesus (Mark 1:8). In fact, he is so determined to make sure people understand that Jesus is truly the One to worship, he tells the crowds that he is merely a stagehand while Jesus is the star of the drama (Mark 1:7). What incredible humility and a powerful example for us!

The Bottom Line

Our entire lives are meant to point others to Jesus.

EXPERIENCE

Complete this sentence: My life points other people to _____.

As we see in John the Baptist's example, God wants our lives to point other people to Jesus. However, our gifts, our desires, and our relationships can get in the way of this calling. You may realize that your life actually points other people to things, hobbies, success, or even yourself instead of Jesus. Now ask someone you trust to complete the sentence for you. Sometimes others can view the results of our actions more clearly than we see them ourselves.

HOW CAN YOUR LIFE POINT OTHERS TO JESUS? CONSIDER YOUR GIFTS, YOUR FRIENDS, YOUR FAMILY, AND YOUR TIME.

Takeaway and Pray

My takeaway from this experience is

My prayer today is a

__ REQUEST __ CONFESSION __ PRAISE

ordinary or extra- ordinary?

Mark 1:16-20; 2:13-17;
3:13-19; 6:7-13

Know before You Go

Jesus chooses His twelve disciples from all different backgrounds.

Read the Passage

¹ ¹⁶⁻¹⁸Passing along the beach of Lake Galilee, he saw Simon and his brother Andrew net-fishing. Fishing was their regular work. Jesus said to them, "Come with me. I'll make a new kind of fisherman out of you. I'll show you how to catch men and women instead of perch and bass." They didn't ask questions. They dropped their nets and followed.

¹⁹⁻²⁰A dozen yards or so down the beach, he saw the brothers James and John, Zebedee's sons. They were in the boat, mending their fishnets. Right off, he made the same offer. Immediately, they left their father Zebedee, the boat, and the hired hands, and followed.

² ¹³⁻¹⁴Then Jesus went again to walk alongside the lake. Again a crowd came to him, and he taught them. Strolling along, he saw Levi, son of Alphaeus, at his work collecting taxes. Jesus said, "Come along with me." He came.

¹⁵⁻¹⁶Later Jesus and his disciples were at home having supper with a collection of disreputable guests. Unlikely as it seems, more than a few of them had become followers. The religion scholars and Pharisees saw him keeping this kind of company and lit into his disciples: "What kind of example is this, acting cozy with the misfits?"

¹⁷Jesus, overhearing, shot back, "Who needs a doctor: the healthy or the sick? I'm here inviting the sin-sick, not the spiritually-fit."

^{3:13-19}He climbed a mountain and invited those he wanted with him. They climbed together. He settled on twelve, and designated them apostles. The plan was that they would be with him, and he would send them out to proclaim the Word and give them authority to banish demons. These are the Twelve:

Simon (Jesus later named him Peter, meaning "Rock"),
James, son of Zebedee,
John, brother of James (Jesus nicknamed the Zebedee brothers Boanerges,
    meaning "Sons of Thunder"),
Andrew,
Philip,
Bartholomew,
Matthew,
Thomas,
James, son of Alphaeus,
Thaddaeus,
Simon the Canaanite,
Judas Iscariot (who betrayed him).

^{6:7-8}Jesus called the Twelve to him, and sent them out in pairs. He gave them authority and power to deal with the evil opposition. He sent them off with these instructions:

8-9"Don't think you need a lot of extra equipment for this. *You* are the equipment. No special appeals for funds. Keep it simple.

10"And no luxury inns. Get a modest place and be content there until you leave.

11"If you're not welcomed, not listened to, quietly withdraw. Don't make a scene. Shrug your shoulders and be on your way."

12-13Then they were on the road. They preached with joyful urgency that life can be radically different; right and left they sent the demons packing; they brought wellness to the sick, anointing their bodies, healing their spirits.

After the Passage

These select passages (we will come back to the passages we skipped in the coming days) describe the group of people Jesus chooses as His first followers—the disciples. Perhaps the most extraordinary thing about Jesus' choice of men is that these men are extremely ordinary. They are not rich, influential, famous, or religiously trained; they are just ordinary people.

In fact, one man Jesus chooses causes quite a controversy—He calls a man named Levi, who is a tax collector (Mark 2:14). Tax collectors are some of the most hated people in Jesus' day, and under no circumstances do people think a person like Levi should be hanging around someone like Jesus. When Jesus is questioned about His choice, He tells the crowd He is not just interested in being around so-called nice or good people (Mark 2:17). The main reason Jesus came to earth is to be with sinful, rude, and even mean people. In this passage, Jesus introduces a new way of thinking that we will see throughout the Gospel of Mark: Everyone needs a Savior. Jesus is going to use ordinary people to communicate this truth!

Though the disciples waste no time in following Jesus—some literally leave right in the middle of their jobs—Mark 6:7-13 shows that this excitement is not just a spur-of-the-moment decision. Well into Jesus' ministry, this group of ordinary men continue to follow Jesus—even if it means giving up everything (Mark 6:8-9). While certainly the disciples and their faith are not perfect, Jesus uses the faith and dedication of these men to do extraordinary things (Mark 6:12-13)!

The Bottom Line

Jesus uses the ordinary to do the extraordinary.

EXPERIENCE

Even before Jesus chooses the disciples, God has a record of using the ordinary to display His power. For example, He uses Moses' ordinary staff to deliver Israel from Egypt, the most powerful nation in the world! God uses a slingshot in the hand of a teenager named David to defeat Goliath—one of the strongest, most feared warriors in history! In these circumstances, including the ministry of the disciples, it is not the power of the object but rather God's power that allows the ordinary to have extraordinary results.

List five things in your life that are very ordinary. Your list could include your school supplies, your chore list, your phone, or something in your house. We use these objects every day in very ordinary ways. Now consider how God could use these things to do the extraordinary. List the possibilities next to your five ordinary things. Let these items be a reminder that through God's power, God can, and does, use ordinary things in the hands of ordinary people to do the extraordinary.

ORDINARY ITEM

EXTRAORDINARY POSSIBILITY

Takeaway and Pray

My takeaway from this experience is

My prayer today is a

__ REQUEST __ CONFESSION __ PRAISE

the healing streak

Mark 1:21-45

Know before You Go

Jesus continues His ministry by miraculously healing people.

Read the Passage

1: 21-22 Then they entered Capernaum. When the Sabbath arrived, Jesus lost no time in getting to the meeting place. He spent the day there teaching. They were surprised at his teaching—so forthright, so confident—not quibbling and quoting like the religion scholars.

23-24 Suddenly, while still in the meeting place, he was interrupted by a man who was deeply disturbed and yelling out, "What business do you have here with us, Jesus? Nazarene! I know what you're up to! You're the Holy One of God, and you've come to destroy us!"

25-26 Jesus shut him up: "Quiet! Get out of him!" The afflicting spirit threw the man into spasms, protesting loudly—and got out.

27-28 Everyone there was spellbound, buzzing with curiosity. "What's going on here? A new teaching that does what it says? He shuts up defiling, demonic spirits and tells them to get lost!" News of this traveled fast and was soon all over Galilee.

²⁹⁻³¹Directly on leaving the meeting place, they came to Simon and Andrew's house, accompanied by James and John. Simon's mother-in-law was sick in bed, burning up with fever. They told Jesus. He went to her, took her hand, and raised her up. No sooner had the fever left than she was up fixing dinner for them.

³²⁻³⁴That evening, after the sun was down, they brought sick and evil-afflicted people to him, the whole city lined up at his door! He cured their sick bodies and tormented spirits. Because the demons knew his true identity, he didn't let them say a word.

³⁵⁻³⁷While it was still night, way before dawn, he got up and went out to a secluded spot and prayed. Simon and those with him went looking for him. They found him and said, "Everybody's looking for you."

³⁸⁻³⁹Jesus said, "Let's go to the rest of the villages so I can preach there also. This is why I've come." He went to their meeting places all through Galilee, preaching and throwing out the demons.

⁴⁰A leper came to him, begging on his knees, "If you want to, you can cleanse me."

⁴¹⁻⁴⁵Deeply moved, Jesus put out his hand, touched him, and said, "I want to. Be clean." Then and there the leprosy was gone, his skin smooth and healthy. Jesus dismissed him with strict orders: "Say nothing to anyone. Take the offering for cleansing that Moses prescribed and present yourself to the priest. This will validate your healing to the people." But as soon as the man was out of earshot, he told everyone he met what had happened, spreading the news all over town. So Jesus kept to out-of-the-way places, no longer able to move freely in and out of the city. But people found him, and came from all over.

After the Passage

Jesus' way of teaching is different from the other teachers' way in His time. He speaks like He has words directly from God—and He does (Mark 1:21-22). In addition to His powerful teaching, Jesus catches people's attention with incredible miracles like the ones Mark describes in this passage.

Both Jesus' teachings and His miracles show His authority over all things (Mark 1:27). This word, *authority*, is important to understand because it is used often in the Gospel of Mark. When a person has authority over something, the person has the power to make decisions or give orders. It is important to understand that authority is also gained by having the correct position. For instance, if your math teacher assigns you homework, then you understand that you should come to class tomorrow with your homework completed. Your teacher has the power, or authority, to give you that instruction. If, however, a math expert who is not your teacher asks you to complete a homework assignment, then you will be less motivated to finish the homework. Why? Because you understand that it's your teacher's *position*, not math knowledge or the skill to do math problems, that carries the necessary authority to assign you homework. Your math teacher is the only person who has authority to assign you math homework.

The same idea is true of Jesus. Jesus has authority because He is the Son of God. He is a good teacher and does incredible miracles, but His authority comes from God. The miracles in Mark 1:21-45 are important because they show that Jesus' authority and power have no limits. He has authority over the spiritual world (e.g., driving out demons) and the physical world (e.g., healing Peter's mother-in-law and the man with leprosy). There has never been, and there never will be, anyone like Jesus—His authority sets Him apart from all of history! He demonstrates this authority in the miracles we read about and can exercise the same authority in your life as well.

The Bottom Line

Jesus' authority has no limits.

EXPERIENCE

Sometimes when we think of authority, we think of it as a negative idea. Teachers assign work to students, children have to obey their parents, the law creates rules to follow, and so on. However, we see through Jesus' example that authority can actually bring about order, healing, and life change.

List the ways the following authority figures help your life.

POSITION	HOW CAN THIS AUTHORITY FIGURE HELP YOU?	HOW IS JESUS' AUTHORITY SIMILAR TO OR DIFFERENT FROM THIS PERSON'S?
Teacher		
Coach		
Police Officer		
Referee		
President		

WHAT PARTS OF YOUR LIFE DO YOU NEED TO SURRENDER TO JESUS' AUTHORITY?

Takeaway and Pray

My takeaway from this experience is

My prayer today is a

___ REQUEST ___ CONFESSION ___ PRAISE

get up
& walk!

Mark 2:1-12

Know before You Go

Jesus shows His authority
when He both heals and
forgives a paralyzed man.

Read the Passage

2:1-5After a few days, Jesus returned to Capernaum, and word got around that he
was back home. A crowd gathered, jamming the entrance so no one could get in or
out. He was teaching the Word. They brought a paraplegic to him, carried by four
men. When they weren't able to get in because of the crowd, they removed part of
the roof and lowered the paraplegic on his stretcher. Impressed by their bold belief,
Jesus said to the paraplegic, "Son, I forgive your sins."

6-7Some religion scholars sitting there started whispering among themselves,
"He can't talk that way! That's blasphemy! God and only God can forgive sins."

8-12Jesus knew right away what they were thinking, and said, "Why are you
so skeptical? Which is simpler: to say to the paraplegic, 'I forgive your sins,' or
say, 'Get up, take your stretcher, and start walking'? Well, just so it's clear that I'm
the Son of Man and authorized to do either, or both . . ." (he looked now at the

paraplegic), "Get up. Pick up your stretcher and go home." And the man did it—got up, grabbed his stretcher, and walked out, with everyone there watching him. They rubbed their eyes, stunned—and then praised God, saying, "We've never seen anything like this!"

After the Passage

Like the leper in the previous chapter, the paralyzed man has incredible faith that Jesus has the power to heal him. After a very dramatic entrance, Jesus says something that surprises, and frustrates, some people in attendance (Mark 2:6-7). Rather than heal the man immediately, Jesus tells the man that his sins are forgiven (Mark 2:5). What prompts Jesus to say this? Forgiveness is not what the man had come for—he wanted the ability to walk! Jesus offers this paralyzed man forgiveness for two reasons:

1. Our greatest need is spiritual, not physical. While this man certainly has a great physical need, Jesus' first priority is to forgive the man of his sins—to set his soul right with God. What good is it to walk physically if you are not walking spiritually with God?

2. Jesus is indeed God! Who else could offer such a bold thing as forgiveness? Perhaps there are others in the region who could heal people. While astounding, it most likely would not have been the first time this crowd saw a healing. But the crowd had never heard someone speak on behalf of God like Jesus does. Jesus is clearly and directly telling the crowds that He is more than a prophet or a faith healer—He Himself is God walking on earth (Mark 2:10-12)! We will see this theme develop in the coming days as we keep reading the Gospel of Mark together.

The Bottom Line

Our greatest need is for our souls to be right with God.

EXPERIENCE

List several basic human needs.

Look back at your list. How many of the needs listed are physical needs? Things like a house, health, or clothes? Why do you think it is easier for us to consider our physical needs before our spiritual needs?

In addition to needs for things like clothes and food, we have spiritual and emotional needs. We all need to be loved by God and others. We need strength to get through hard times. We need courage to do the right thing. We need peace when life is stressful. While less obvious, our spiritual needs are just as real as our physical needs.

WHAT SPIRITUAL NEED DO YOU HAVE TODAY? PRAY AND ASK GOD TO MEET THIS NEED.

Takeaway and Pray

My takeaway from this experience is

My prayer today is a

__ REQUEST __ CONFESSION __ PRAISE

everything has changed

Mark 2:18–3:12, 20-35

Know before You Go

We will be introduced to several religious laws and traditions from the Old Testament in these passages.

Read the Passage

2:18The disciples of John and the disciples of the Pharisees made a practice of fasting. Some people confronted Jesus: "Why do the followers of John and the Pharisees take on the discipline of fasting, but your followers don't?"

19-20Jesus said, "When you're celebrating a wedding, you don't skimp on the cake and wine. You feast. Later you may need to pull in your belt, but not now. As long as the bride and groom are with you, you have a good time. No one throws cold water on a friendly bonfire. This is Kingdom Come!"

21-22He went on, "No one cuts up a fine silk scarf to patch old work clothes; you want fabrics that match. And you don't put your wine in cracked bottles."

23-24One Sabbath day he was walking through a field of ripe grain. As his disciples made a path, they pulled off heads of grain. The Pharisees told on them to Jesus: "Look, your disciples are breaking Sabbath rules!"

25-28 Jesus said, "Really? Haven't you ever read what David did when he was hungry, along with those who were with him? How he entered the sanctuary and ate fresh bread off the altar, with the Chief Priest Abiathar right there watching— holy bread that no one but priests were allowed to eat—and handed it out to his companions?" Then Jesus said, "The Sabbath was made to serve us; we weren't made to serve the Sabbath. The Son of Man is no yes-man to the Sabbath. He's in charge!"

3:1-3 Then he went back in the meeting place where he found a man with a crippled hand. The Pharisees had their eyes on Jesus to see if he would heal him, hoping to catch him in a Sabbath violation. He said to the man with the crippled hand, "Stand here where we can see you."

4 Then he spoke to the people: "What kind of action suits the Sabbath best? Doing good or doing evil? Helping people or leaving them helpless?" No one said a word.

5-6 He looked them in the eye, one after another, angry now, furious at their hard-nosed religion. He said to the man, "Hold out your hand." He held it out—it was as good as new! The Pharisees got out as fast as they could, sputtering about how they would join forces with Herod's followers and ruin him.

7-10 Jesus went off with his disciples to the sea to get away. But a huge crowd from Galilee trailed after them—also from Judea, Jerusalem, Idumea, across the Jordan, and around Tyre and Sidon—swarms of people who had heard the reports and had come to see for themselves. He told his disciples to get a boat ready so he wouldn't be trampled by the crowd. He had healed many people, and now everyone who had something wrong was pushing and shoving to get near and touch him.

11-12 Evil spirits, when they recognized him, fell down and cried out, "You are the Son of God!" But Jesus would have none of it. He shut them up, forbidding them to identify him in public.

3:20-21 Jesus came home and, as usual, a crowd gathered—so many making demands on him that there wasn't even time to eat. His friends heard what was going on and went to rescue him, by force if necessary. They suspected he was believing his own press.

22-27The religion scholars from Jerusalem came down spreading rumors that he was working black magic, using devil tricks to impress them with spiritual power. Jesus confronted their slander with a story: "Does it make sense to send a devil to catch a devil, to use Satan to get rid of Satan? A constantly squabbling family disintegrates. If Satan were fighting Satan, there soon wouldn't be any Satan left. Do you think it's possible in broad daylight to enter the house of an awake, able-bodied man, and walk off with his possessions unless you tie him up first? Tie him up, though, and you can clean him out.

28-30"Listen to this carefully. I'm warning you. There's nothing done or said that can't be forgiven. But if you persist in your slanders against God's Holy Spirit, you are repudiating the very One who forgives, sawing off the branch on which you're sitting, severing by your own perversity all connection with the One who forgives." He gave this warning because they were accusing him of being in league with Evil.

31-32Just then his mother and brothers showed up. Standing outside, they relayed a message that they wanted a word with him. He was surrounded by the crowd when he was given the message, "Your mother and brothers and sisters are outside looking for you."

33-35Jesus responded, "Who do you think are my mother and brothers?" Looking around, taking in everyone seated around him, he said, "Right here, right in front of you—my mother and my brothers. Obedience is thicker than blood. The person who obeys God's will is my brother and sister and mother."

After the Passage

This group of passages can be a bit tricky to understand—fasting (Mark 2:18-20), garments and wineskins (Mark 2:21-22), the Sabbath and Abiathar the Chief Priest (Mark 2:23–3:6), and Satan and eternal sin (Mark 3:20-34)—what does it all mean? Without getting too overwhelmed by the details, let us consider the major themes and lessons in these passages.

The law from the Old Testament included rules for people to follow. For example, there were instructions about fasting: not eating for a period of time to show focus, commitment, and dedication to God (Mark 2:18-20). There were guidelines for what someone could do and not do on the Sabbath, God's holy day (Mark 2:23-28). These rules helped people understand who was following God and who was not—the rules were a few of the many ways that people interacted with God and were set apart from those who subscribed to other religions.

But with Jesus and His Good News, everything changes! Jesus tells people the primary way to interact with God is now through a relationship with Jesus—not through a set of traditions, rules, and rituals. Jesus is trying to help the people understand that, while those rules were not bad or evil, they were never meant to be a substitute for a genuine relationship with God. Unfortunately, many religious leaders (called the Pharisees) would prioritize following these rules over loving God.

The Bottom Line

Rules, rituals, and traditions are no substitute for a genuine relationship with God.

EXPERIENCE

Find something in your house that you can easily and safely remove the batteries from—something like a flashlight or remote. With the batteries removed, try to turn on the object. Any luck? Of course not—the batteries have been removed! Now put the batteries back in and try again—everything works, right?

It does not make sense for you to use a flashlight without batteries—it will not work. It also does not make sense to do religious things without a real relationship with Jesus. The Pharisees' rules and traditions, like fasting, are like a flashlight without the batteries. Their actions are not bad—they are just pointless unless they extend from a real love for God.

How can you avoid acting like a Pharisee in your relationship with God?

What types of actions are a temptation for you to do without a real relationship with God?

How can you use actions to actually draw near to God?

Takeaway and Pray

My takeaway from this experience is

My prayer today is a

__ REQUEST __ CONFESSION __ PRAISE

the parables
of good news

Mark 4:1-34

Know before You Go

This chapter includes four
parables, or stories, about
people's possible responses
to Jesus' teachings.

Read the Passage

^{4:1-2}He went back to teaching by the sea. A crowd built up to such a great size that
he had to get into an offshore boat, using the boat as a pulpit as the people pushed
to the water's edge. He taught by using stories, many stories.

³⁻⁸"Listen. What do you make of this? A farmer planted seed. As he scattered
the seed, some of it fell on the road and birds ate it. Some fell in the gravel; it
sprouted quickly but didn't put down roots, so when the sun came up it withered
just as quickly. Some fell in the weeds; as it came up, it was strangled among the
weeds and nothing came of it. Some fell on good earth and came up with a flourish,
producing a harvest exceeding his wildest dreams.

⁹"Are you listening to this? Really listening?"

¹⁰⁻¹²When they were off by themselves, those who were close to him, along with
the Twelve, asked about the stories. He told them, "You've been given insight into

God's kingdom—you know how it works. But to those who can't see it yet, everything comes in stories, creating readiness, nudging them toward a welcome awakening. These are people—

Whose eyes are open but don't see a thing,
Whose ears are open but don't understand a word,
Who avoid making an about-face and getting forgiven."

[13]He continued, "Do you see how this story works? All my stories work this way. [14-15]"The farmer plants the Word. Some people are like the seed that falls on the hardened soil of the road. No sooner do they hear the Word than Satan snatches away what has been planted in them.

[16-17]"And some are like the seed that lands in the gravel. When they first hear the Word, they respond with great enthusiasm. But there is such shallow soil of character that when the emotions wear off and some difficulty arrives, there is nothing to show for it.

[18-19]"The seed cast in the weeds represents the ones who hear the kingdom news but are overwhelmed with worries about all the things they have to do and all the things they want to get. The stress strangles what they heard, and nothing comes of it.

[20]"But the seed planted in the good earth represents those who hear the Word, embrace it, and produce a harvest beyond their wildest dreams."

[21-22]Jesus went on: "Does anyone bring a lamp home and put it under a bucket or beneath the bed? Don't you put it up on a table or on the mantel? We're not keeping secrets, we're telling them; we're not hiding things, we're bringing them out into the open.

[23]"Are you listening to this? Really listening?

[24-25]"Listen carefully to what I am saying—and be wary of the shrewd advice that tells you how to get ahead in the world on your own. Giving, not getting, is the way. Generosity begets generosity. Stinginess impoverishes."

²⁶⁻²⁹Then Jesus said, "God's kingdom is like seed thrown on a field by a man who then goes to bed and forgets about it. The seed sprouts and grows—he has no idea how it happens. The earth does it all without his help: first a green stem of grass, then a bud, then the ripened grain. When the grain is fully formed, he reaps—harvest time!

³⁰⁻³²"How can we picture God's kingdom? What kind of story can we use? It's like an acorn. When it lands on the ground it is quite small as seeds go, yet once it is planted it grows into a huge oak tree with thick branches. Eagles nest in it."

³³⁻³⁴With many stories like these, he presented his message to them, fitting the stories to their experience and maturity. He was never without a story when he spoke. When he was alone with his disciples, he went over everything, sorting out the tangles, untying the knots.

After the Passage

Mark 4 introduces us to one of Jesus' favorite teaching methods—parables. Parables are stories that use common, everyday images, like nature, family, or money, to explain a truth about God, salvation, or the Christian life. In Mark 4:1-20, Jesus uses a very familiar task to His audience, spreading seeds, to explain how different people respond to the gospel. Some have no interest (the path in Mark 4:4, 15), some are interested at first but quickly lose focus (the rocky soil in Mark 4:5-6, 16-17), some lose faith after life becomes too difficult (the thorny soil in Mark 4:7, 18-19), and some fully accept the gospel (the good soil in Mark 4:8, 20).

Although most people typically focus on the different types of soil when they read Mark 4:1-20, maybe we should pay a little more attention to the role of the farmer. Regardless of the type of soil on which the seeds fall, the farmer's job is to keep throwing seed! In addition to a lesson about the hearts of people and their responses to the gospel, this parable is a reminder that we should continuously share the Good News of Jesus with people—even if people do not always respond in the way that we hope. Keep spreading the news about Jesus! Just as the farmer cannot change the soil in the parable, we cannot control the hearts of those who hear the gospel—only

Jesus can. Our job is to keep spreading the news in the hopes that God will soften the hearts of those who hear it!

The parables that follow in this chapter (the lamp on the table or mantel in Mark 4:21-25 and the acorn in Mark 4:30-34) further explain the parable of the sower. Our responsibility is to share the Good News of salvation, not hide it or keep it to ourselves. As we spread the Good News, we never know how God may use those seeds of truth in someone's life.

The Bottom Line

While we cannot control the condition of people's hearts, we can continue to tell people about Jesus.

EXPERIENCE

While sharing the Good News of Jesus can sometimes be scary, it may be as simple as telling someone that you are reading your Bible and what you are learning. It may be praying with one of your friends or inviting them to come to church with you. Perhaps it is telling someone in your life "God loves you and wants you to have a relationship with Him."

REMEMBER, WE ARE
ONLY RESPONSIBLE FOR
THROWING THE SEED!
ASK GOD TO GIVE YOU THE
COURAGE TO OVERCOME
ANY FEARS YOU MAY HAVE.

Who do you hope to share the Good News with today?

How do you think you might do it?

Takeaway and Pray

My takeaway from this experience is

My prayer today is a

__ REQUEST __ CONFESSION __ PRAISE

calming the chaos

Mark 4:35–5:20

Know before You Go

The next section of Mark continues to show that Jesus is not only a wise prophet or good teacher but indeed God!

Read the Passage

4:35-38Late that day he said to them, "Let's go across to the other side." They took him in the boat as he was. Other boats came along. A huge storm came up. Waves poured into the boat, threatening to sink it. And Jesus was in the stern, head on a pillow, sleeping! They roused him, saying, "Teacher, is it nothing to you that we're going down?"

39-40Awake now, he told the wind to pipe down and said to the sea, "Quiet! Settle down!" The wind ran out of breath; the sea became smooth as glass. Jesus reprimanded the disciples: "Why are you such cowards? Don't you have any faith at all?"

41They were in absolute awe, staggered. "Who is this, anyway?" they asked. "Wind and sea at his beck and call!"

5:1-5They arrived on the other side of the sea in the country of the Gerasenes. As Jesus got out of the boat, a madman from the cemetery came up to him. He lived there among the tombs and graves. No one could restrain him—he couldn't be chained, couldn't be tied down. He had been tied up many times with chains and ropes, but he broke the chains, snapped the ropes. No one was strong enough to tame him. Night and day he roamed through the graves and the hills, screaming out and slashing himself with sharp stones.

6-8When he saw Jesus a long way off, he ran and bowed in worship before him—then howled in protest, "What business do you have, Jesus, Son of the High God, messing with me? I swear to God, don't give me a hard time!" (Jesus had just commanded the tormenting evil spirit, "Out! Get out of the man!")

9-10Jesus asked him, "Tell me your name."

He replied, "My name is Mob. I'm a rioting mob." Then he desperately begged Jesus not to banish them from the country.

11-13A large herd of pigs was grazing and rooting on a nearby hill. The demons begged him, "Send us to the pigs so we can live in them." Jesus gave the order. But it was even worse for the pigs than for the man. Crazed, they stampeded over a cliff into the sea and drowned.

14-15Those tending the pigs, scared to death, bolted and told their story in town and country. Everyone wanted to see what had happened. They came up to Jesus and saw the madman sitting there wearing decent clothes and making sense, no longer a walking madhouse of a man.

16-17Those who had seen it told the others what had happened to the demon-possessed man and the pigs. At first they were in awe—and then they were upset, upset over the drowned pigs. They demanded that Jesus leave and not come back.

18-20As Jesus was getting into the boat, the demon-delivered man begged to go along, but he wouldn't let him. Jesus said, "Go home to your own people. Tell them your story—what the Master did, how he had mercy on you." The man went back and began to preach in the Ten Towns area about what Jesus had done for him. He was the talk of the town.

After the Passage

The story of the disciples in the boat is a reminder that even in the midst of life's storms, Jesus is present (Mark 4:35-41). The disciples are afraid—and they have every right to be! To be in the middle of a lake during a violent storm would be terrifying. What they do not realize, however, is that Jesus is God over everything—including creation and the weather! Despite their fear and lack of faith, Jesus delivers them from their near disaster (Mark 4:39). Interestingly, even after Jesus demonstrates His power over creation, the disciples are still unsure of who He is and why He has such power (Mark 4:40-41).

When Jesus and the disciples safely arrive at the other side of the lake, they are met by a crazy, demon-possessed man—a man who is a danger to himself as well as the rest of the town (Mark 5:1-5). He is, in every sense of the phrase, out of control. As Jesus does in the previous story, He shows His control over creation and heals the man of his demon possession (Mark 5:6-15). For the second time in a matter of hours, Jesus brings order to chaos. He brings peace to a frightening situation!

Note: If this passage or others about demon possession frighten you, take comfort in the fact that Jesus is way more powerful than the evil He faces in every scenario described in the Gospel of Mark. If you are following Jesus, there is no need to fear!

The Bottom Line

Jesus has the power to bring order to chaos.

EXPERIENCE

ILLUSTRATE WHAT CHAOS LOOKS LIKE FOR YOU

ILLUSTRATE WHAT ORDER LOOKS LIKE FOR YOU

WHAT ONE AREA OF YOUR LIFE THAT IS IN CHAOS DO YOU WISH JESUS WOULD BRING ORDER TO? PRAY AND ASK GOD FOR THIS PEACE.

Takeaway and Pray

My takeaway from this experience is

My prayer today is a

__ REQUEST __ CONFESSION __ PRAISE

all in time

Mark 5:21-43

Know before You Go

This passage includes two miracles that Jesus performs in response to people's faith.

Read the Passage

5:21-24 After Jesus crossed over by boat, a large crowd met him at the seaside. One of the meeting-place leaders named Jairus came. When he saw Jesus, he fell to his knees, beside himself as he begged, "My dear daughter is at death's door. Come and lay hands on her so she will get well and live." Jesus went with him, the whole crowd tagging along, pushing and jostling him.

25-29 A woman who had suffered a condition of hemorrhaging for twelve years—a long succession of physicians had treated her, and treated her badly, taking all her money and leaving her worse off than before—had heard about Jesus. She slipped in from behind and touched his robe. She was thinking to herself, "If I can put a finger on his robe, I can get well." The moment she did it, the flow of blood dried up. She could feel the change and knew her plague was over and done with.

³⁰At the same moment, Jesus felt energy discharging from him. He turned around to the crowd and asked, "Who touched my robe?"

³¹His disciples said, "What are you talking about? With this crowd pushing and jostling you, you're asking, 'Who touched me?' Dozens have touched you!"

³²⁻³³But he went on asking, looking around to see who had done it. The woman, knowing what had happened, knowing she was the one, stepped up in fear and trembling, knelt before him, and gave him the whole story.

³⁴Jesus said to her, "Daughter, you took a risk of faith, and now you're healed and whole. Live well, live blessed! Be healed of your plague."

^{5:35}While he was still talking, some people came from the leader's house and told him, "Your daughter is dead. Why bother the Teacher any more?"

³⁶Jesus overheard what they were talking about and said to the leader, "Don't listen to them; just trust me."

³⁷⁻⁴⁰He permitted no one to go in with him except Peter, James, and John. They entered the leader's house and pushed their way through the gossips looking for a story and neighbors bringing in casseroles. Jesus was abrupt: "Why all this busybody grief and gossip? This child isn't dead; she's sleeping." Provoked to sarcasm, they told him he didn't know what he was talking about.

⁴⁰⁻⁴³But when he had sent them all out, he took the child's father and mother, along with his companions, and entered the child's room. He clasped the girl's hand and said, "*Talitha koum*," which means, "Little girl, get up." At that, she was up and walking around! This girl was twelve years of age. They, of course, were all beside themselves with joy. He gave them strict orders that no one was to know what had taken place in that room. Then he said, "Give her something to eat."

After the Passage

The story of Jairus's daughter and the sick woman is yet another powerful example of faith in the Gospel of Mark. The story begins with a religious man named Jairus, who has tremendous faith. He truly believes that if Jesus is willing, He can heal his severely ill daughter (Mark 5:22-23). After agreeing to see Jairus's daughter, Jesus is interrupted by a sick woman who has similar faith to Jairus (Mark 5:25-28). She has been sick for over a decade, and years of seeing doctors have not healed her. Despite her sickness, she believes that Jesus has the power to heal her. In fact, her faith is so strong that just by touching Jesus' garment, she is completely healed of her longtime illness (Mark 5:34)!

While this reality is remarkable news for the sick woman, Jairus's daughter passes away while Jesus interacts with the woman. Hope is lost—Jairus's household thinks that Jesus has not responded in time (Mark 5:35). Despite the seemingly hopeless situation, Jesus still travels to Jairus's house, where his family and friends are mourning the passing of the young girl. In an incredible scene, Jesus brings the girl back to life—and orders her something to eat (Mark 5:41-43)!

As we see in this passage, God's plan is often different from our plans. In the hearts and minds of everyone involved in this scene, Jesus is too late in His response to Jairus's need. No one can possibly blame them for thinking this way—Jairus's daughter has passed away, so they assume that is final. Jesus, however, has another plan in mind. His plan involves an even more incredible display of power and healing, but His timeline is different from what the people expected.

Sometimes when we seek God, we need to remember that He operates in His time and according to His plan. God never forgets about you or runs late accidentally—He has a purpose and appropriate time for everything. Accepting God's timing and plan, however, requires faith from us! We need to remember that no situation is ever hopeless. No matter what hardship you are facing, God is able to use the situation to show His power. Never give up faith!

The Bottom Line

God's plan and timing are perfect but often different from ours.

EXPERIENCE

What is one situation, person, or circumstance that it seems like God has forgotten about?

What do you wish God would do in that situation? Write it down and then ask Him to do it today.

What can you learn about God or yourself as you wait for His response?

PICK A RANDOM TIME OF DAY—ANY TIME. MAYBE IT IS 8:12 OR 10:19. EVERY DAY AT THAT TIME, REMIND YOURSELF THAT GOD'S TIMING IS PERFECT.

Takeaway and Pray

My takeaway from this experience is

My prayer today is a

___ REQUEST ___ CONFESSION ___ PRAISE

your Christian status

Mark 6:1-6, 14-29

Know before You Go

Jesus returns to His hometown, and the people do not respond well. Also, sadly, we learn about the graphic death of John the Baptist.

Read the Passage

6:1-2He left there and returned to his hometown. His disciples came along. On the Sabbath, he gave a lecture in the meeting place. He stole the show, impressing everyone. "We had no idea he was this good!" they said. "How did he get so wise all of a sudden, get such ability?"

3But in the next breath they were cutting him down: "He's just a carpenter— Mary's boy. We've known him since he was a kid. We know his brothers, James, Justus, Jude, and Simon, and his sisters. Who does he think he is?" They tripped over what little they knew about him and fell, sprawling. And they never got any further.

4-6Jesus told them, "A prophet has little honor in his hometown, among his relatives, on the streets he played in as a child." Jesus wasn't able to do much of anything there—he laid hands on a few sick people and healed them, that's all.

He couldn't get over their stubbornness. He left and made a circuit of the other villages, teaching.

⬩

6:14King Herod heard of all this, for by this time the name of Jesus was on everyone's lips. He said, "This has to be John the Baptizer come back from the dead—that's why he's able to work miracles!"

15Others said, "No, it's Elijah."

Others said, "He's a prophet, just like one of the old-time prophets."

16But Herod wouldn't budge: "It's John, sure enough. I cut off his head, and now he's back, alive."

17-20Herod was the one who had ordered the arrest of John, put him in chains, and sent him to prison at the nagging of Herodias, his brother Philip's wife. For John had provoked Herod by naming his relationship with Herodias "adultery." Herodias, smoldering with hate, wanted to kill him, but didn't dare because Herod was in awe of John. Convinced that he was a holy man, he gave him special treatment. Whenever he listened to him he was miserable with guilt—and yet he couldn't stay away. Something in John kept pulling him back.

21-22But a portentous day arrived when Herod threw a birthday party, inviting all the brass and bluebloods in Galilee. Herodias's daughter entered the banquet hall and danced for the guests. She charmed Herod and the guests.

22-23The king said to the girl, "Ask me anything. I'll give you anything you want." Carried away, he kept on, "I swear, I'll split my kingdom with you if you say so!"

24She went back to her mother and said, "What should I ask for?"

"Ask for the head of John the Baptizer."

25Excited, she ran back to the king and said, "I want the head of John the Baptizer served up on a platter. And I want it now!"

26-29That sobered the king up fast. But unwilling to lose face with his guests, he caved in and let her have her wish. The king sent the executioner off to the prison with orders to bring back John's head. He went, cut off John's head, brought it back on a platter, and presented it to the girl, who gave it to her mother. When John's disciples heard about this, they came and got the body and gave it a decent burial.

After the Passage

The events in Mark 5 tell of two people, the sick woman and Jairus, who have never met Jesus but have complete faith in His power and ability to heal. The events in Mark 6 tell of people who flat-out reject Jesus' words and miracles—the people in Jesus' home-town! These people knew Jesus as a young boy and are very familiar with His life story, yet they are skeptical of His claims and power.

Mark 6:1-6 serves as a humble reminder that being around Jesus does not automati-cally result in belief, trust, and faith. The crowds in Jesus' hometown prove this truth—sometimes those most familiar with Jesus can miss the most important fact about Him: He is the Savior (Mark 6:4-6)! Knowledge of Jesus is dangerously different from faith in Jesus. Faith requires a response that knowledge does not. We sometimes dangerously assume that being around Christian things, like church or Christian friends, will develop our faith for us.

It is appropriate to be a bit bothered by the story of John the Baptist's death in Mark 6:14-29. His beheading in the last part of this chapter is cruel, yet it serves as an example of how the message of Jesus often angers people (Mark 6:19-24). Two thou-sand years later, many people still struggle to understand and accept the words of Jesus; some may even find them offensive. Because of this reaction, we should not be surprised if we encounter opposition when we follow Jesus and actively put our faith in Him.

The Bottom Line

Knowledge of Jesus is dangerously different from faith in Jesus.

EXPERIENCE

List the different things people do if they are Christians.

Of all the things that people do if they are Christians, the only thing that guarantees salvation is faith and trust in Jesus Christ. All other actions are a result of that faith, not a substitute for it.

How do you keep a relationship with Jesus at the center of your actions?

If you have been relying on your Christian actions but have never put your faith in Jesus, consider trusting Him with your life today. Take the time to pray this prayer or something like it:

God, I understand that knowledge of You and faith in You are two different things. I want to put my faith in You and follow You each day of my life. Please forgive me of my sins. Thank You for offering salvation through Your Son, Jesus Christ. Help me understand what it means to keep You at the center of my actions each day.

Takeaway and Pray

My takeaway from this experience is

My prayer today is a

__ REQUEST __ CONFESSION __ PRAISE

no
limits

Mark 6:30-56

Know before You Go

This passage includes two
of the most well-known stories
of Jesus: the feeding of five
thousand people and Jesus
walking on water.

Read the Passage

^{6:30-31}The apostles then rendezvoused with Jesus and reported on all that they had done and taught. Jesus said, "Come off by yourselves; let's take a break and get a little rest." For there was constant coming and going. They didn't even have time to eat.

³²⁻³⁴So they got in the boat and went off to a remote place by themselves. Someone saw them going and the word got around. From the surrounding towns people went out on foot, running, and got there ahead of them. When Jesus arrived, he saw this huge crowd. At the sight of them, his heart broke—like sheep with no shepherd they were. He went right to work teaching them.

³⁵⁻³⁶When his disciples thought this had gone on long enough—it was now quite late in the day—they interrupted: "We are a long way out in the country, and it's

very late. Pronounce a benediction and send these folks off so they can get some supper."

[37]Jesus said, "You do it. Fix supper for them."

They replied, "Are you serious? You want us to go spend a fortune on food for their supper?"

[38]But he was quite serious. "How many loaves of bread do you have? Take an inventory."

That didn't take long. "Five," they said, "plus two fish."

[39-44]Jesus got them all to sit down in groups of fifty or a hundred—they looked like a patchwork quilt of wildflowers spread out on the green grass! He took the five loaves and two fish, lifted his face to heaven in prayer, blessed, broke, and gave the bread to the disciples, and the disciples in turn gave it to the people. He did the same with the fish. They all ate their fill. The disciples gathered twelve baskets of leftovers. More than five thousand were at the supper.

[45-46]As soon as the meal was finished, Jesus insisted that the disciples get in the boat and go on ahead across to Bethsaida while he dismissed the congregation. After sending them off, he climbed a mountain to pray.

[47-49]Late at night, the boat was far out at sea; Jesus was still by himself on land. He could see his men struggling with the oars, the wind having come up against them. At about four o'clock in the morning, Jesus came toward them, walking on the sea. He intended to go right by them. But when they saw him walking on the sea, they thought it was a ghost and screamed, scared to death.

[50-52]Jesus was quick to comfort them: "Courage! It's me. Don't be afraid." As soon as he climbed into the boat, the wind died down. They were stunned, shaking their heads, wondering what was going on. They didn't understand what he had done at the supper. None of this had yet penetrated their hearts.

[53-56]They beached the boat at Gennesaret and tied up at the landing. As soon as they got out of the boat, word got around fast. People ran this way and that, bringing their sick on stretchers to where they heard he was. Wherever he went, village or town or country crossroads, they brought their sick to the marketplace and begged him to let them touch the edge of his coat—that's all. And whoever touched him became well.

After the Passage

While much attention is rightly given to these miraculous acts, perhaps even more astounding is the care and compassion Jesus shows the people in these two miracles. In Mark 6:30-44, Jesus interacts with a crowd of people and notices their deeply spiritual needs. They are hurting. They are lost. They are in need of a leader. In response to their spiritual needs, Jesus feels compassion for them (Mark 6:34). Perhaps this compassion is the reason for the miracle. Jesus is able to meet their spiritual needs by first meeting their physical need: supper. If Jesus does not feed the crowd, the people will go home to eat and miss the opportunity to be with Jesus. Feeding the crowd supper keeps them in Jesus' presence, and they therefore receive the love and care they need from their Shepherd.

Similarly, while Jesus is praying alone, He sees His disciples struggling in the middle of the sea. In another act of compassion and care, He walks out to them on the water and calms the sea (Mark 6:47-52). In both instances, the physical acts of Jesus are awesome—both miracles show His incredible power over the world He created. While we often focus on the miracles, do not miss the reason for them. It seems that Jesus' motivation behind both miracles is to show care and compassion to those around Him.

The Bottom Line

Jesus' compassion has no limits. Nothing can stop Jesus from loving us deeply!

EXPERIENCE

Read Romans 8:38-39. What do these verses say about God's love for us?

Look in the mirror. How do you see yourself? List the words that come to mind when you see the reflection looking back at you.

These two miracles remind us that Jesus not only sees us but also loves us deeply. Write the numbers *6:34* and *6:50* on a sticky note, and place it on your mirror. These two verses in Mark 6 tell us that Jesus sees and cares about His people.

LET THE STICKY NOTE SERVE AS A REMINDER THAT JESUS SEES YOU AND CARES ABOUT YOU!

Takeaway and Pray

My takeaway from this experience is

My prayer today is a

__ REQUEST __ CONFESSION __ PRAISE

heart
of the
matter

Mark 7:1-23

Know before You Go

Jesus addresses another tradition from the Old Testament: In order to honor God, people choose to ceremonially wash their hands before they eat, but Jesus explains how this tradition has changed and also addresses an important truth.

Read the Passage

7:1-4 The Pharisees, along with some religion scholars who had come from Jerusalem, gathered around him. They noticed that some of his disciples weren't being careful with ritual washings before meals. The Pharisees—Jews in general, in fact—would never eat a meal without going through the motions of a ritual hand-washing, with an especially vigorous scrubbing if they had just come from the market (to say nothing of the scourings they'd give jugs and pots and pans).

5 The Pharisees and religion scholars asked, "Why do your disciples brush off the rules, showing up at meals without washing their hands?"

6-8 Jesus answered, "Isaiah was right about frauds like you, hit the bull's-eye in fact:

> These people make a big show of saying the right thing,
>   but their heart isn't in it.
> They act like they are worshiping me,
>   but they don't mean it.
> They just use me as a cover
>   for teaching whatever suits their fancy,
> Ditching God's command
>   and taking up the latest fads."

9-13 He went on, "Well, good for you. You get rid of God's command so you won't be inconvenienced in following the religious fashions! Moses said, 'Respect your father and mother,' and, 'Anyone denouncing father or mother should be killed.' But you weasel out of that by saying that it's perfectly acceptable to say to father or mother, 'Gift! What I owed you I've given as a gift to God,' thus relieving yourselves of obligation to father or mother. You scratch out God's Word and scrawl a whim in its place. You do a lot of things like this."

14-15 Jesus called the crowd together again and said, "Listen now, all of you—take this to heart. It's not what you swallow that pollutes your life; it's what you vomit—that's the real pollution."

17 When he was back home after being with the crowd, his disciples said, "We don't get it. Put it in plain language."

18-19 Jesus said, "Are you being willfully stupid? Don't you see that what you swallow can't contaminate you? It doesn't enter your heart but your stomach, works its way through the intestines, and is finally flushed." (That took care of dietary quibbling; Jesus was saying that *all* foods are fit to eat.)

20-23 He went on: "It's what comes out of a person that pollutes: obscenities, lusts, thefts, murders, adulteries, greed, depravity, deceptive dealings, carousing, mean looks, slander, arrogance, foolishness—all these are vomit from the heart. *There* is the source of your pollution."

After the Passage

The conversation about handwashing between Jesus and the Pharisees in Mark 7 is not about germs or hygiene. The conversation centers around the way a person becomes holy in the eyes of God. These religious leaders have created an extra set of rules in order to protect themselves from breaking God's law. This ceremonial washing is a layer of protection from becoming unholy (Mark 7:3-5). While the heart behind these additional routines may have been pure at first, these man-made rules have eventually come to seem just as important as God's original instructions (Mark 7:8). This shift is exactly what has happened with the washing of hands in this scene. This washing is a tradition, or a preference, created by the Pharisees, not a commandment from God. Nonetheless, the religious leaders heavily judge and condemn those who do not follow their man-made traditions of washing.

A modern-day example of this tradition is the dress code for church. While there is nothing wrong with wearing nice clothes to church, nowhere in the Bible does God give us a dress code for worship. You can love God and wear shorts just as easily as you can wear nice clothes and have no relationship with Him (Mark 7:6-8). It would be wrong for you to judge someone for wearing shorts to church or claim they are not a Christian because of their style of dress. This type of judgment would have been common of the Pharisees.

The issue with these types of traditions and preferences is that they are completely external and do not reflect the true condition of our hearts. Jesus is more concerned about our hearts and the resulting actions toward God and others (Mark 7:20-23).

The Bottom Line

Jesus cares deeply about the condition of our hearts.

EXPERIENCE

Make a timeline of your day yesterday. Include some of your actions and interactions with others.

What was the motivation behind some of your actions yesterday? Did your actions stem from love, respect, or care for others? Or did they stem from selfishness, judgment, or anger? Explain.

NOW GO WASH YOUR HANDS.

Every time you wash your hands today (which is hopefully a lot!), remind yourself that God is more concerned with the condition of your heart than He is with the condition of your hands. Each day is a new opportunity to understand this important truth.

Takeaway and Pray

My takeaway from this experience is

My prayer today is a

__ REQUEST __ CONFESSION __ PRAISE

an open invite

Mark 7:24-37

Know before You Go

Jesus often performs miracles for people who are rejected and judged by the surrounding communities.

Read the Passage

^{7:24-26}From there Jesus set out for the vicinity of Tyre. He entered a house there where he didn't think he would be found, but he couldn't escape notice. He was barely inside when a woman who had a disturbed daughter heard where he was. She came and knelt at his feet, begging for help. The woman was Greek, Syro-Phoenician by birth. She asked him to cure her daughter.

²⁷He said, "Stand in line and take your turn. The children get fed first. If there's any left over, the dogs get it."

²⁸She said, "Of course, Master. But don't dogs under the table get scraps dropped by the children?"

²⁹⁻³⁰Jesus was impressed. "You're right! On your way! Your daughter is no longer disturbed. The demonic affliction is gone." She went home and found her daughter relaxed on the bed, the torment gone for good.

³¹⁻³⁵Then he left the region of Tyre, went through Sidon back to Galilee Lake and over to the district of the Ten Towns. Some people brought a man who could neither hear nor speak and asked Jesus to lay a healing hand on him. He took the man off by himself, put his fingers in the man's ears and some spit on the man's tongue. Then Jesus looked up in prayer, groaned mightily, and commanded, "*Ephphatha!*— Open up!" And it happened. The man's hearing was clear and his speech plain—just like that.

³⁶⁻³⁷Jesus urged them to keep it quiet, but they talked it up all the more, beside themselves with excitement. "He's done it all and done it well. He gives hearing to the deaf, speech to the speechless."

After the Passage

These two interactions once again show the compassion of Jesus—first to a non-Jewish woman (Mark 7:24-30) and second to a man who can neither hear nor speak (Mark 7:31-37). Both of these individuals represent outcasts in Jewish society. The woman is Greek—or more importantly, not Jewish. She does not belong. Even as an outcast, she has faith—incredible faith! Jesus is amazed by her faith and therefore extends healing to her daughter (Mark 7:29-30). Similarly, in dramatic fashion, Jesus heals the deaf and mute man at the request of the man's friends (Mark 7:32-35).

Unfortunately, sometimes we think it is impossible for certain people to know Jesus. For one reason or another, we tend to assume that Jesus cares for a specific group of people. If we are honest with ourselves, this group of people look and act a lot like we do. Stories like the ones in Mark 7:24-37 remind us that Jesus is available to anyone who has faith. No one in your life, or in the entire world, is outside the reach of Jesus! Regardless of a person's birthplace, appearance, language, education, status, wealth, health, or even view of God, Jesus desires to have a relationship with everyone.

The Bottom Line

The Good News of Jesus is for everyone.

EXPERIENCE

Be like Jesus today and reach out to someone who seems to be an outsider. Talk to them, invite them to lunch with your friends, ask them some questions, and get to know them. Sometimes a simple act can go a long way to make someone feel loved!

AS YOU REFLECT ON THIS INTERACTION, HOW WERE YOU LIKE JESUS TO THIS OUTSIDER TODAY?

Takeaway and Pray

My takeaway from this experience is

My prayer today is a

__ REQUEST   __ CONFESSION   __ PRAISE

an encore

Mark 8:1-12

Know before You Go

Once again, Jesus has compassion for a group of people. This time He feeds a crowd of four thousand people who have been with Him for three days.

Read the Passage

^{8:1-3} At about this same time he again found himself with a hungry crowd on his hands. He called his disciples together and said, "This crowd is breaking my heart. They have stuck with me for three days, and now they have nothing to eat. If I send them home hungry, they'll faint along the way—some of them have come a long distance."

⁴ His disciples responded, "What do you expect us to do about it? Buy food out here in the desert?"

⁵ He asked, "How much bread do you have?"

"Seven loaves," they said.

⁶⁻¹⁰ So Jesus told the crowd to sit down on the ground. After giving thanks, he took the seven bread loaves, broke them into pieces, and gave them to his disciples so they could hand them out to the crowd. They also had a few fish. He pronounced

a blessing over the fish and told his disciples to hand them out as well. The crowd ate its fill. Seven sacks of leftovers were collected. There were well over four thousand at the meal. Then he sent them home. He himself went straight to the boat with his disciples and set out for Dalmanoutha.

¹¹⁻¹²When they arrived, the Pharisees came out and started in on him, badgering him to prove himself, pushing him up against the wall. Provoked, he said, "Why does this generation clamor for miraculous guarantees? If I have anything to say about it, you'll not get so much as a hint of a guarantee."

After the Passage

This situation is remarkably similar to the one involving the crowd of five thousand mentioned in Mark 6. Unfortunately, the disciples react similarly here. When the time comes to feed the crowd, the disciples express the same concern as before. They ask Jesus how they can possibly feed such a massive crowd (Mark 8:4). While we do not know exactly how much time passed between these two miraculous feedings, the disciples could not have forgotten this previous miracle, could they? Where is the disciples' faith? Where is their confidence in Jesus' power that He has previously shown in this exact same situation?

While we are quick to mock the disciples for their lack of understanding, how often do we forget God's power in our own lives? Even after God shows Himself to be faithful to us, we start to doubt Him in our very next challenge. Remembering God's goodness in our past helps us have faith in our present circumstances. The disciples forget Jesus' power and ability to meet the very need He has previously met. The Pharisees also ask Jesus for a sign from heaven right after witnessing an amazing testament to His power (Mark 8:11-12). Both the disciples and the Pharisees need more assurance for their faith even though the faithfulness they have experienced in the past should have been enough.

The Bottom Line

Remembering God's actions in the past is a key to our hope for the future.

EXPERIENCE

Make a list of the ways God has been faithful in your life. Consider previous doubts, fears, or worries you used to have.

IN THE PAST WEEK	IN THE PAST MONTH	IN THE PAST YEAR

HOW DOES REMEMBERING GOD'S FAITHFULNESS IN THE PAST HELP YOU HAVE FAITH FOR THE FUTURE?

Takeaway and Pray

My takeaway from this experience is

My prayer today is a

___ REQUEST ___ CONFESSION ___ PRAISE

motions over motive

Mark 8:13-26

Know before You Go

This passage includes a stern warning to the disciples not to follow the teachings of the Pharisees.

Read the Passage

8:13-15He then left them, got back in the boat, and headed for the other side. But the disciples forgot to pack a lunch. Except for a single loaf of bread, there wasn't a crumb in the boat. Jesus warned, "Be very careful. Keep a sharp eye out for the contaminating yeast of Pharisees and the followers of Herod."

16-19Meanwhile, the disciples were finding fault with each other because they had forgotten to bring bread. Jesus overheard and said, "Why are you fussing because you forgot bread? Don't you see the point of all this? Don't you get it at all? Remember the five loaves I broke for the five thousand? How many baskets of leftovers did you pick up?"

They said, "Twelve."

²⁰"And the seven loaves for the four thousand—how many bags full of leftovers did you get?"

"Seven."

²¹He said, "Do you still not get it?"

²²⁻²³They arrived at Bethsaida. Some people brought a sightless man and begged Jesus to give him a healing touch. Taking him by the hand, he led him out of the village. He put spit in the man's eyes, laid hands on him, and asked, "Do you see anything?"

²⁴⁻²⁶He looked up. "I see men. They look like walking trees." So Jesus laid hands on his eyes again. The man looked hard and realized that he had recovered perfect sight, saw everything in bright, twenty-twenty focus. Jesus sent him straight home, telling him, "Don't enter the village."

After the Passage

As a reminder, the Pharisees are the religious leaders we discussed earlier in our reading of the Gospel of Mark. They are more concerned with rules and regulations than with a relationship with God. In Mark 8:15, Jesus calls the Pharisees yeast—a powerful ingredient found in bread that makes it rise when baked. Just a small amount of yeast can completely change the makings of the bread. Jesus uses this image immediately after His miracle involving thousands of loaves of bread—this connection of yeast to loaves should help the disciples understand His warning. The teaching of the Pharisees is like yeast in bread: Their thinking completely and wrongly changes how people interact with God.

The warning remains relevant for us today. Although the actual Pharisees no longer exist, there are certainly people in our lives who think like the Pharisees. These negative influences can be rather deceiving. At first glance, Pharisee-minded people seem very connected to God and His teachings. However, their commitment to religion only affects their actions and does not challenge their hearts. Pharisee-minded people can distract us from the heart of Jesus' teaching by tempting us to focus solely on the rules and traditions of religion. Pharisee-minded people miss the very point of the gospel.

The Bottom Line

Our relationship with God can become distorted when we prioritize the motions over the motive.

EXPERIENCE

In Mark 8:22, Jesus meets a blind man from Bethsaida. This town is known for being a cruel and unwelcoming community. Like the Pharisees, the people there lack faith and doubt Jesus' power. Because of their thoughts toward Jesus, He chooses to heal the blind man outside Bethsaida (Mark 8:23) and tells the man not to return to the village after He heals him (Mark 8:26). Although this command from Jesus seems harsh, it illustrates how negative of an influence Pharisee-minded people can have on believers.

What or who in your life do you need to separate from to strengthen your relationship with God? This object, activity, or person may not be entirely bad, but its influence could be negatively impacting your life.

PRAY TO GOD AND
ASK FOR CLARITY AND
STRENGTH AS YOU
CONSIDER SEPARATING
YOURSELF FROM THIS
INFLUENCE.

Takeaway and Pray

My takeaway from this experience is

My prayer today is a

__ REQUEST __ CONFESSION __ PRAISE

who am I?

Mark 8:27-33

Know before You Go

These verses illustrate how Peter, a disciple of Jesus, understands Jesus' identity but not His significance.

Read the Passage

8:27 Jesus and his disciples headed out for the villages around Caesarea Philippi. As they walked, he asked, "Who do the people say I am?"

28 "Some say 'John the Baptizer,'" they said. "Others say 'Elijah.' Still others say 'one of the prophets.'"

29 He then asked, "And you—what are you saying about me? Who am I?"

Peter gave the answer: "You are the Christ, the Messiah."

30-32 Jesus warned them to keep it quiet, not to breathe a word of it to anyone. He then began explaining things to them: "It is necessary that the Son of Man proceed to an ordeal of suffering, be tried and found guilty by the elders, high priests, and religion scholars, be killed, and after three days rise up alive." He said this simply and clearly so they couldn't miss it.

³²⁻³³But Peter grabbed him in protest. Turning and seeing his disciples wavering, wondering what to believe, Jesus confronted Peter. "Peter, get out of my way! Satan, get lost! You have no idea how God works."

After the Passage

As you can imagine, Jesus is extremely popular during His time on earth. As He heals the sick, walks on water, and raises people from the dead, people start to notice Him. Furthermore, the message He preaches is different than the words of the religious leaders—and this difference is refreshing to hear.

His teachings and ministry make Jesus highly controversial. People have a difficult time drawing conclusions about His identity—who is Jesus? Is He a prophet like the prophets of the Old Testament (Mark 8:28)? Is He just a controversial rabbi? Some think He is even crazy! Aware of this confusion around town, Jesus asks His disciples who they think He is. In other words, Jesus is asking His disciples to draw a conclusion for themselves.

Although we have seen the disciples stumble in the past, Peter has incredible faith and answers profoundly in this moment. He states that Jesus is the Messiah (Mark 8:29). However, Peter has yet to understand the significance of Jesus' role as the Messiah (Mark 8:32-33). He does not understand that Jesus' ministry on earth is more than performing miracles and healing sick people—His role as the Messiah has the higher calling of the Cross.

Two thousand years later, people still have all sorts of opinions about Jesus, but the question still remains for you personally: Who do you say Jesus is? This question is the most important question you could ever answer.

The Bottom Line

You must answer Jesus' question for yourself: "And you—what are you saying about me? Who am I?" (Mark 8:29).

EXPERIENCE

List some important people in your life. Who do they say Jesus is?

WHO DO YOU SAY JESUS IS?

Takeaway and Pray

My takeaway from this experience is

My prayer today is a

__ REQUEST __ CONFESSION __ PRAISE

old self to new self

Mark 8:34–9:29

Know before You Go

Jesus explains the possible responses a person can have to the gospel. Furthermore, Jesus shows three disciples His power. Finally, Jesus heals a possessed boy.

Read the Passage

8:34-37Calling the crowd to join his disciples, he said, "Anyone who intends to come with me has to let me lead. You're not in the driver's seat; *I* am. Don't run from suffering; embrace it. Follow me and I'll show you how. Self-help is no help at all. Self-sacrifice is the way, my way, to saving yourself, your true self. What good would it do to get everything you want and lose you, the real you? What could you ever trade your soul for?

38"If any of you are embarrassed over me and the way I'm leading you when you get around your fickle and unfocused friends, know that you'll be an even greater embarrassment to the Son of Man when he arrives in all the splendor of God, his Father, with an army of the holy angels."

9:1Then he drove it home by saying, "This isn't pie in the sky by and by. Some of you who are standing here are going to see it happen, see the kingdom of God arrive in full force."

²⁻⁴Six days later, three of them *did* see it. Jesus took Peter, James, and John and led them up a high mountain. His appearance changed from the inside out, right before their eyes. His clothes shimmered, glistening white, whiter than any bleach could make them. Elijah, along with Moses, came into view, in deep conversation with Jesus.

⁵⁻⁶Peter interrupted, "Rabbi, this is a great moment! Let's build three memorials—one for you, one for Moses, one for Elijah." He blurted this out without thinking, stunned as they all were by what they were seeing.

⁷Just then a light-radiant cloud enveloped them, and from deep in the cloud, a voice: "This is my Son, marked by my love. Listen to him."

⁸The next minute the disciples were looking around, rubbing their eyes, seeing nothing but Jesus, only Jesus.

⁹⁻¹⁰Coming down the mountain, Jesus swore them to secrecy. "Don't tell a soul what you saw. After the Son of Man rises from the dead, you're free to talk." They puzzled over that, wondering what on earth "rising from the dead" meant.

¹¹Meanwhile they were asking, "Why do the religion scholars say that Elijah has to come first?"

¹²⁻¹³Jesus replied, "Elijah does come first and get everything ready for the coming of the Son of Man. They treated this Elijah like dirt, much like they will treat the Son of Man, who will, according to Scripture, suffer terribly and be kicked around contemptibly."

¹⁴⁻¹⁶When they came back down the mountain to the other disciples, they saw a huge crowd around them, and the religion scholars cross-examining them. As soon as the people in the crowd saw Jesus, admiring excitement stirred them. They ran and greeted him. He asked, "What's going on? What's all the commotion?"

¹⁷⁻¹⁸A man out of the crowd answered, "Teacher, I brought my mute son, made speechless by a demon, to you. Whenever it seizes him, it throws him to the ground. He foams at the mouth, grinds his teeth, and goes stiff as a board. I told your disciples, hoping they could deliver him, but they couldn't."

¹⁹⁻²⁰Jesus said, "What a generation! No sense of God! How many times do I have to go over these things? How much longer do I have to put up with this? Bring the boy here." They brought him. When the demon saw Jesus, it threw the boy into a seizure, causing him to writhe on the ground and foam at the mouth.

[21-22]He asked the boy's father, "How long has this been going on?"

"Ever since he was a little boy. Many times it pitches him into fire or the river to do away with him. If you can do anything, do it. Have a heart and help us!"

[23]Jesus said, "If? There are no 'ifs' among believers. Anything can happen."

[24]No sooner were the words out of his mouth than the father cried, "Then I believe. Help me with my doubts!"

[25-27]Seeing that the crowd was forming fast, Jesus gave the vile spirit its marching orders: "Dumb and deaf spirit, I command you—Out of him, and stay out!" Screaming, and with much thrashing about, it left. The boy was pale as a corpse, so people started saying, "He's dead." But Jesus, taking his hand, raised him. The boy stood up.

[28]After arriving back home, his disciples cornered Jesus and asked, "Why couldn't we throw the demon out?"

[29]He answered, "There is no way to get rid of this kind of demon except by prayer."

After the Passage

Although several interactions occur in these passages, the words of Jesus in Mark 8:34-38 and 9:1 are where we will focus our attention. Jesus' call to His people to let Him lead (see Mark 8:34) could define how you live your entire life.

As we read in Mark 8:29, Peter realizes that Jesus is the Messiah. Mark 8:34-8:38 and 9:1 then explain how we should respond to this reality. If we choose to believe that Jesus is the Messiah, then this choice requires that we don't run from suffering but instead follow Jesus and let Him be in the driver's seat (Mark 8:34). You lose your old life and exchange it for a new life (Mark 8:35). In other words, the person you were before you knew Jesus should be completely different from the person you are after choosing to follow Jesus.

The person you were before Jesus was first concerned about yourself—your comfort, your money, your relationships, and your status. Your focus was entirely on how you could become the greatest, wealthiest, and most successful person during your years on earth. However, Jesus reminds us that gaining the whole world makes no difference if you have not decided to follow Him (Mark 8:36-38).

When you choose to follow Jesus, the focus of your life is now on Jesus. You are no longer focused on yourself but rather focused on serving others, becoming humble, being generous, and showing others God's grace. Someone who truly follows Jesus realizes that this life on earth is temporary but the next life in heaven is forever.

The statements Jesus makes at the end of this chapter should cause you to stop and reflect. If you have made the decision to follow Jesus, Mark 8:34-38 and 9:1 should motivate you to deny your old self daily and live according to Jesus' command. This choice may even cause you to make some sacrifices, but Jesus assures us that it is worth it in the end!

The Bottom Line

Our lives should be radically different when we follow Jesus.

EXPERIENCE

Draw two people: one who represents your old life and one who represents your new life. Write ideas or things that each self prioritizes around each drawing. Consider what should be different about these two people. You may not remember your life before Jesus, so consider the difference between an earthly focus and a heavenly focus.

OLD SELF | NEW SELF

WHAT CHOICES ARE YOU MAKING TO DENY YOUR OLD SELF AND TO FOCUS YOUR LIFE ON JESUS?

Takeaway and Pray

My takeaway from this experience is

My prayer today is a

__ REQUEST __ CONFESSION __ PRAISE

warnings ahead

Mark 9:30-50

Know before You Go

These passages include some bizarre instructions for followers of Jesus. The word pictures Jesus uses help us understand what Christians should prioritize in their walks with God.

Read the Passage

9:30-32 Leaving there, they went through Galilee. He didn't want anyone to know their whereabouts, for he wanted to teach his disciples. He told them, "The Son of Man is about to be betrayed to some people who want nothing to do with God. They will murder him. Three days after his murder, he will rise, alive." They didn't know what he was talking about, but were afraid to ask him about it.

33They came to Capernaum. When he was safe at home, he asked them, "What were you discussing on the road?"

34The silence was deafening—they had been arguing with one another over who among them was greatest.

35He sat down and summoned the Twelve. "So you want first place? Then take the last place. Be the servant of all."

³⁶⁻³⁷He put a child in the middle of the room. Then, cradling the little one in his arms, he said, "Whoever embraces one of these children as I do embraces me, and far more than me—God who sent me."

^{9:38}John spoke up, "Teacher, we saw a man using your name to expel demons and we stopped him because he wasn't in our group."

³⁹⁻⁴¹Jesus wasn't pleased. "Don't stop him. No one can use my name to do something good and powerful, and in the next breath slam me. If he's not an enemy, he's an ally. Why, anyone by just giving you a cup of water in my name is on our side. Count on it that God will notice.

⁴²"On the other hand, if you give one of these simple, childlike believers a hard time, bullying or taking advantage of their simple trust, you'll soon wish you hadn't. You'd be better off dropped in the middle of the lake with a millstone around your neck.

⁴³⁻⁴⁸"If your hand or your foot gets in God's way, chop it off and throw it away. You're better off maimed or lame and alive than the proud owner of two hands and two feet, godless in a furnace of eternal fire. And if your eye distracts you from God, pull it out and throw it away. You're better off one-eyed and alive than exercising your twenty-twenty vision from inside the fire of hell.

⁴⁹⁻⁵⁰"Everyone's going through a refining fire sooner or later, but you'll be well-preserved, protected from the *eternal* flames. Be preservatives yourselves. Preserve the peace."

After the Passage

Jesus' words at the end of Mark 9 are a great example of hyperbole. Hyperbole is when someone uses an extreme exaggeration to make a point. It would be like telling your mom after coming home from summer camp "I am so tired I could sleep for days." You, of course, are not making a scientific claim about the number of hours you plan to rest, and your mom would certainly not expect you to sleep for forty-eight hours straight. While you are not necessarily using accurate details, you are being accurate in describing the principle—you are extremely exhausted. If you said, "Summer camp was a lot of fun—I am pretty tired," your mom may not fully understand just how tired you are. Because you said "I could sleep for days," she now knows not to plan any family dinners or activities because you need some serious rest!

Jesus uses this type of speech in His teaching on temptation and sin in Mark 9:42-50. His point is not to start chopping off body parts; rather, Jesus further illustrates that the things of this world are temporary and worth far less than our souls (as we just read in Mark 8:34-38 and 9:1). In other words, it is better to limp after Jesus than run after the world. If something is hurting our relationship with Jesus, we should do whatever we can to get rid of it—even if it requires extreme action!

The Bottom Line

Your relationship with Jesus is valuable and worth protecting at all costs.

EXPERIENCE

Many things can hurt your relationship with Jesus. Certain things tempt us and lead us into a pattern of sin. Some things distract us by taking up too much time in our schedules. Others, even if they are good things, become too big of a priority in our lives. All these things, even if for different reasons, can impact our relationship with Jesus.

What are some of these things for you?

What are some extreme ways to handle them, and what are some realistic ways to handle them?

THINGS THAT HURT MY RELATIONSHIP WITH JESUS	HYPERBOLIC SOLUTION	PRACTICAL SOLUTION
Example: my phone	throw my phone off the roof	limit the amount of time I spend on my phone

Takeaway and Pray

My takeaway from this experience is

My prayer today is a

__ REQUEST __ CONFESSION __ PRAISE

our greatest possession

Mark 10:1-31

Know before You Go

Jesus interacts with several people who are familiar with the Old Testament law. He challenges their interpretations of this law and explains how the gospel changes the law's application.

Read the Passage

¹⁰:¹⁻²From there he went to the area of Judea across the Jordan. A crowd of people, as was so often the case, went along, and he, as he so often did, taught them. Pharisees came up, intending to give him a hard time. They asked, "Is it legal for a man to divorce his wife?"

³Jesus said, "What did Moses command?"

⁴They answered, "Moses gave permission to fill out a certificate of dismissal and divorce her."

⁵⁻⁹Jesus said, "Moses wrote this command only as a concession to your hardhearted ways. In the original creation, God made male and female to be together. Because of this, a man leaves father and mother, and in marriage he becomes one flesh with a woman—no longer two individuals, but forming a new

unity. Because God created this organic union of the two sexes, no one should desecrate his art by cutting them apart."

¹⁰⁻¹²When they were back home, the disciples brought it up again. Jesus gave it to them straight: "A man who divorces his wife so he can marry someone else commits adultery against her. And a woman who divorces her husband so she can marry someone else commits adultery."

¹⁰:¹³⁻¹⁶The people brought children to Jesus, hoping he might touch them. The disciples shooed them off. But Jesus was irate and let them know it: "Don't push these children away. Don't ever get between them and me. These children are at the very center of life in the kingdom. Mark this: Unless you accept God's kingdom in the simplicity of a child, you'll never get in." Then, gathering the children up in his arms, he laid his hands of blessing on them.

¹⁷As he went out into the street, a man came running up, greeted him with great reverence, and asked, "Good Teacher, what must I do to get eternal life?"

¹⁸⁻¹⁹Jesus said, "Why are you calling me good? No one is good, only God. You know the commandments: Don't murder, don't commit adultery, don't steal, don't lie, don't cheat, honor your father and mother."

²⁰He said, "Teacher, I have—from my youth—kept them all!"

²¹Jesus looked him hard in the eye—and loved him! He said, "There's one thing left: Go sell whatever you own and give it to the poor. All your wealth will then be heavenly wealth. And come follow me."

²²The man's face clouded over. This was the last thing he expected to hear, and he walked off with a heavy heart. He was holding on tight to a lot of things, and not about to let go.

²³⁻²⁵Looking at his disciples, Jesus said, "Do you have any idea how difficult it is for people who 'have it all' to enter God's kingdom?" The disciples couldn't believe what they were hearing, but Jesus kept on: "You can't imagine how difficult. I'd say it's easier for a camel to go through a needle's eye than for the rich to get into God's kingdom."

²⁶*That* got their attention. "Then who has any chance at all?" they asked.

²⁷Jesus was blunt: "No chance at all if you think you can pull it off by yourself. Every chance in the world if you let God do it."

²⁸Peter tried another angle: "We left everything and followed you."

²⁹⁻³¹Jesus said, "Mark my words, no one who sacrifices house, brothers, sisters, mother, father, children, land—whatever—because of me and the Message will lose out. They'll get it all back, but multiplied many times in homes, brothers, sisters, mothers, children, and land—but also in troubles. And then the bonus of eternal life! This is once again the Great Reversal: Many who are first will end up last, and the last first."

After the Passage

Jesus' interaction with the rich man in Mark 10:17-31 continues to highlight the theme that we see in the Gospel of Mark: Nothing on this earth is worth more than a relationship with Jesus. Do you remember some of the other examples of this theme? Jesus tells His disciples that following Him means that they are to take up their cross daily and asks them the thought-provoking question "What good would it do to get everything you want and lose you, the real you? What could you ever trade your soul for?" (Mark 8:36-37). Later, He explains that even our hands, feet, and eyes are not worth more than following Jesus (Mark 9:42-50).

In Mark 10:20, the rich man tells Jesus that he has kept every commandment from the Old Testament. This feat is highly unlikely—no one could keep the entire law. Jesus does not confront the rich man's obvious lie. Rather, Jesus suggests a rather bold action to expose the condition of the rich man's heart: Jesus tells him to sell everything and then follow Him (Mark 10:21). The man's reaction reveals exactly what Jesus is trying to explain. He follows the rules to gain wealth and influence on earth, not to experience a relationship with God.

The rich man leaves Jesus without understanding Jesus' point (Mark 10:22). Jesus then explains to His disciples that the rich have a hard time seeing their need for Jesus because wealth meets most of their physical needs (Mark 10:23-25). Money or stuff is not evil; however, it can distract us from seeing that Jesus is the most important thing in life and the only way to meet our greater, spiritual needs (Mark 10:27-31).

Are Jesus' instructions to the rich man the same instructions to us? Are we supposed to sell everything in order to follow Jesus? Not necessarily. His instructions to the man are to expose that the man's heart is far from God and far too attached to this world. While Jesus' instructions are not exactly meant for us, the principle behind His question still applies to us. Is our priority this world or Jesus?

The Bottom Line

Jesus should be our number one priority in life.

EXPERIENCE

For the rich man, money was the object that he put above a relationship with Jesus. While it may not be money for you, there are likely a few things in your life that you are tempted to love more than Jesus.

Illustrate three things in your life that would be hard for you to give up if Jesus commanded you to.

WATCH OUT FOR THESE THINGS! WHILE THESE THINGS ARE LIKELY NOT BAD, THEY MAY BECOME MORE IMPORTANT THAN JESUS IF YOU ARE NOT CAREFUL.

Takeaway and Pray

My takeaway from this experience is

My prayer today is a

__ REQUEST __ CONFESSION __ PRAISE

first or last?

Mark 10:32-52

Know before You Go

Jesus cares for His sometimes-selfish disciples by predicting His upcoming death and explaining the importance of service. He also heals a blind man who is overlooked by many.

Read the Passage

10:32-34Back on the road, they set out for Jerusalem. Jesus had a head start on them, and they were following, puzzled and not just a little afraid. He took the Twelve and began again to go over what to expect next. "Listen to me carefully. We're on our way up to Jerusalem. When we get there, the Son of Man will be betrayed to the religious leaders and scholars. They will sentence him to death. Then they will hand him over to the Romans, who will mock and spit on him, give him the third degree, and kill him. After three days he will rise alive."

35James and John, Zebedee's sons, came up to him. "Teacher, we have something we want you to do for us."

36"What is it? I'll see what I can do."

37"Arrange it," they said, "so that we will be awarded the highest places of honor in your glory—one of us at your right, the other at your left."

38Jesus said, "You have no idea what you're asking. Are you capable of drinking the cup I drink, of being baptized in the baptism I'm about to be plunged into?"

³⁹⁻⁴⁰"Sure," they said. "Why not?"

Jesus said, "Come to think of it, you *will* drink the cup I drink, and be baptized in my baptism. But as to awarding places of honor, that's not my business. There are other arrangements for that."

⁴¹⁻⁴⁵When the other ten heard of this conversation, they lost their tempers with James and John. Jesus got them together to settle things down. "You've observed how godless rulers throw their weight around," he said, "and when people get a little power how quickly it goes to their heads. It's not going to be that way with you. Whoever wants to be great must become a servant. Whoever wants to be first among you must be your slave. That is what the Son of Man has done: He came to serve, not to be served—and then to give away his life in exchange for many who are held hostage."

^{10:46-48}They spent some time in Jericho. As Jesus was leaving town, trailed by his disciples and a parade of people, a blind beggar by the name of Bartimaeus, son of Timaeus, was sitting alongside the road. When he heard that Jesus the Nazarene was passing by, he began to cry out, "Son of David, Jesus! Mercy, have mercy on me!" Many tried to hush him up, but he yelled all the louder, "Son of David! Mercy, have mercy on me!"

⁴⁹⁻⁵⁰Jesus stopped in his tracks. "Call him over."

They called him. "It's your lucky day! Get up! He's calling you to come!" Throwing off his coat, he was on his feet at once and came to Jesus.

⁵¹Jesus said, "What can I do for you?"

The blind man said, "Rabbi, I want to see."

⁵²"On your way," said Jesus. "Your faith has saved and healed you."

In that very instant he recovered his sight and followed Jesus down the road.

After the Passage

The disciples are often slow in their understanding of Jesus' messages. For example, in Mark 10:31, Jesus tells His disciples that the first will end up last in the Kingdom of God. What happens just a few verses later? The disciples start arguing about who will be first and who will get to be the most powerful person in heaven (Mark 10:37)! The disciples clearly misunderstand the mission of Jesus, which is to promote the Kingdom of God, not to make people powerful.

When Jesus says "Many who are first will end up last, and the last first" (Mark 10:31), He is not saying that everyone who has ever been last in line will be first in line in heaven. Jesus simply means that the gospel changes everything. Everything we value on earth does not matter when it comes to following Jesus—He turns our earthly priorities upside down. The world values being strong; Jesus values acknowledging our weakness. The world values being rich; Jesus values removing distractions. The world values popularity; Jesus values everyone knowing His name. The world values selfish power; Jesus values humble service. Jesus changes everything. Our mission in life does not center around ourselves; it centers around Jesus and pointing people to Him as we serve others (Mark 10:42-45).

In Mark 10:51, Jesus asks the blind man Bartimaeus, "What can I do for you?" He asks essentially the same question to the disciples in Mark 10:36. The disciples answer that they want Him to make them great, and Jesus does not grant their request. The blind man, however, simply answers, "I want to see," and Jesus heals the man. The different answers to the same question serve as yet more examples of Jesus' radical priorities: Jesus models His commandment and serves the blind, poor beggar (Mark 10:52). The request of His disciples to be great simply does not align with Jesus' mission on earth!

The Bottom Line

The most powerful people in the kingdom of God are humble servants.

EXPERIENCE

Serve someone today.

Memorize Mark 10:45: "That is what the Son of Man has done: He came to serve, not to be served—and then to give away his life in exchange for many who are held hostage."

Takeaway and Pray

My takeaway from this experience is

My prayer today is a

__ REQUEST __ CONFESSION __ PRAISE

a humble entrance

Mark 11:1-11

Know before You Go

In ancient times, a king's grand entrance into the temple was a very important moment, because the temple was the most important building in town. In this passage, we experience Jesus' entry into the Temple of Jerusalem.

Read the Passage

11:1-3When they were nearing Jerusalem, at Bethphage and Bethany on Mount Olives, he sent off two of the disciples with instructions: "Go to the village across from you. As soon as you enter, you'll find a colt tethered, one that has never yet been ridden. Untie it and bring it. If anyone asks, 'What are you doing?' say, 'The Master needs him, and will return him right away.'"

4-7They went and found a colt tied to a door at the street corner and untied it. Some of those standing there said, "What are you doing untying that colt?" The disciples replied exactly as Jesus had instructed them, and the people let them alone. They brought the colt to Jesus, spread their coats on it, and he mounted.

⁸⁻¹⁰The people gave him a wonderful welcome, some throwing their coats on the street, others spreading out rushes they had cut in the fields. Running ahead and following after, they were calling out,

> Hosanna!
> Blessed is he who comes in God's name!
> Blessed the coming kingdom of our father David!
> Hosanna in highest heaven!

¹¹He entered Jerusalem, then entered the Temple. He looked around, taking it all in. But by now it was late, so he went back to Bethany with the Twelve.

After the Passage

The events in these verses take place a week before Easter—the Sunday now known as Palm Sunday. Jesus is at the height of His popularity—everyone in town knows of His teachings and miracles. When word spreads that Jesus is coming to town to celebrate the Jewish holidays, crowds start to form in order to get a glimpse of Jesus. When Jesus walks by, the crowds yell *hosanna*, which is a word used to worship a savior (Mark 11:9-10). They indeed believe that Jesus is going to be their savior; however, they do not understand how and from what Jesus is going to save them. The expectation of the crowds is that Jesus is going to do something extraordinary in the coming week—perhaps even lead a revolution to take back their city from the Romans!

We see multiple times in the Gospel of Mark that Jesus challenges the way people think about everything. Though He is as popular as ever, He does not use a chariot with majestic stallions and musicians. He rides into town on a borrowed donkey (Mark 11:2, 7). And when He finally arrives at His destination, the Temple, nothing happens. No rally. No speech. He simply turns around and goes home.

This humble entrance should alert the crowds that Jesus is not going to start the revolution they want. Jesus is the Savior from their sin, not from the Roman government. Jesus' death on a cross just a week after His humble entrance into the city is infinitely better than anything the crowds could be hoping for. Unfortunately, the crowds do not understand this truth, and they abandon Jesus in the coming days.

The Bottom Line

Jesus' plan can exceed our most hopeful expectations.

EXPERIENCE

What are some of your biggest hopes? For your life? For your family? For your friends?

If your hopes become your reality, how will your life change?

NOW DREAM WITH
JESUS IN MIND.
HOW CAN JESUS
TRANSFORM YOUR
HOPES TO SHOW
PEOPLE HIS POWER?

Takeaway and Pray

My takeaway from this experience is

My prayer today is a

__ REQUEST __ CONFESSION __ PRAISE

righteous anger

Mark 11:12–12:12

Know before You Go

During Jesus' time in Jerusalem, He faces opposition when He rebukes the religious leaders for making the Temple a marketplace, challenges their unbelief, and tells a parable that foreshadows their rejection of Jesus, the Son of God.

Read the Passage

11:12-14 As they left Bethany the next day, he was hungry. Off in the distance he saw a fig tree in full leaf. He came up to it expecting to find something for breakfast, but found nothing but fig leaves. (It wasn't yet the season for figs.) He addressed the tree: "No one is going to eat fruit from you again—ever!" And his disciples overheard him.

15-17 They arrived at Jerusalem. Immediately on entering the Temple Jesus started throwing out everyone who had set up shop there, buying and selling. He kicked over the tables of the bankers and the stalls of the pigeon merchants. He didn't let anyone even carry a basket through the Temple. And then he taught them, quoting this text:

My house was designated a house of prayer for the nations;
You've turned it into a hangout for thieves.

[18]The high priests and religion scholars heard what was going on and plotted how they might get rid of him. They panicked, for the entire crowd was carried away by his teaching.

[19]At evening, Jesus and his disciples left the city.

[20-21]In the morning, walking along the road, they saw the fig tree, shriveled to a dry stick. Peter, remembering what had happened the previous day, said to him, "Rabbi, look—the fig tree you cursed is shriveled up!"

[22-25]Jesus was matter-of-fact: "Embrace this God-life. Really embrace it, and nothing will be too much for you. This mountain, for instance: Just say, 'Go jump in the lake'—no shuffling or hemming and hawing—and it's as good as done. That's why I urge you to pray for absolutely everything, ranging from small to large. Include everything as you embrace this God-life, and you'll get God's everything. And when you assume the posture of prayer, remember that it's not all *asking*. If you have anything against someone, *forgive*—only then will your heavenly Father be inclined to also wipe your slate clean of sins."

[27-28]Then when they were back in Jerusalem once again, as they were walking through the Temple, the high priests, religion scholars, and leaders came up and demanded, "Show us your credentials. Who authorized you to speak and act like this?"

[29-30]Jesus responded, "First let me ask you a question. Answer my question and then I'll present my credentials. About the baptism of John—who authorized it: heaven or humans? Tell me."

[31-33]They were on the spot, and knew it. They pulled back into a huddle and whispered, "If we say 'heaven,' he'll ask us why we didn't believe John; if we say 'humans,' we'll be up against it with the people because they all hold John up as a prophet." They decided to concede that round to Jesus. "We don't know," they said.

Jesus replied, "Then I won't answer your question either."

[12:1-2]Then Jesus started telling them stories. "A man planted a vineyard. He fenced it, dug a winepress, erected a watchtower, turned it over to the farmhands, and went off on a trip. At the time for harvest, he sent a servant back to the farmhands to collect his profits.

3-5"They grabbed him, beat him up, and sent him off empty-handed. So he sent another servant. That one they tarred and feathered. He sent another and that one they killed. And on and on, many others. Some they beat up, some they killed.

6"Finally there was only one left: a beloved son. In a last-ditch effort, he sent him, thinking, 'Surely they will respect my son.'

7-8"But those farmhands saw their chance. They rubbed their hands together in greed and said, 'This is the heir! Let's kill him and have it all for ourselves.' They grabbed him, killed him, and threw him over the fence.

9-11"What do you think the owner of the vineyard will do? Right. He'll come and get rid of everyone. Then he'll assign the care of the vineyard to others. Read it for yourselves in Scripture:

That stone the masons threw out
    is now the cornerstone!
This is God's work;
    we rub our eyes—we can hardly believe it!"

12They wanted to lynch him then and there but, intimidated by public opinion, held back. They knew the story was about them. They got away from there as fast as they could.

After the Passage

A day after Jesus' celebratory entrance into the city (Mark 11:1-11), Jesus rebukes the money changers in the Temple courts who are profiting from people's worship experiences (Mark 11:15-17). The money changers are charging people for the animals they need to sacrifice to God in the Temple. This scam is like paying ten dollars for a toothbrush at the airport. A toothbrush does not cost ten dollars, but airport vendors take advantage of your forgetfulness and now limited options. However, the money changers' upcharging is a much worse scam because they are making money off God's commands to worship Him at the Temple. Jesus' anger is righteous!

Jesus' interactions in Mark 11 and 12 are the final straw for the religious leaders.

For many months, the religious leaders have been frustrated by Jesus' teaching and the popularity of His message (Mark 11:18). Jesus' message is not only a different message but actually calls their teaching wrong (see Mark 12:12). For generations, these religious leaders have been the spiritual authority for their people. They were the ones who told people what rules to follow and how to interact with God.

Understandably, the religious leaders feel incredibly threatened. The new message of Jesus makes them less powerful, important, and influential. Their solution is to eliminate Jesus by killing Him in hopes of stopping His message. The parable in Mark 12:1-12 is Jesus' sharp warning to the Pharisees who are planning to kill Him. Jesus references the Old Testament as well, showing the religious leaders that He Himself is the cornerstone of the Christian faith (Mark 12:10-11). Rather than listening to the warning and believing Jesus, the religious leaders grow more angry (Mark 12:12).

The Bottom Line

Jesus' message of truth can be controversial.

EXPERIENCE

Look through your music and pick your five favorite songs. What advice are the song lyrics telling you as the listener? List the songs' messages below.

SONG	MESSAGE

SONG	MESSAGE

Are the messages similar to Jesus' message of truth? Why or why not?

BE AWARE OF THE
MESSAGES YOU
ARE ALLOWING TO
INFORM YOUR LIFE.

Takeaway and Pray

My takeaway from this experience is

My prayer today is a

__ REQUEST   __ CONFESSION   __ PRAISE

love God, love others

Mark 12:13-34

Know before You Go

The religious leaders try to trick Jesus by asking Him questions from three categories: tax laws, marriage laws, and Old Testament laws. If Jesus answers their questions incorrectly, they can discredit His message.

Read the Passage

12:13-14They sent some Pharisees and followers of Herod to bait him, hoping to catch him saying something incriminating. They came up and said, "Teacher, we know you have integrity, that you are indifferent to public opinion, don't pander to your students, and teach the way of God accurately. Tell us: Is it lawful to pay taxes to Caesar or not?"

15-16He knew it was a trick question, and said, "Why are you playing these games with me? Bring me a coin and let me look at it." They handed him one.

"This engraving—who does it look like? And whose name is on it?"

"Caesar," they said.

17Jesus said, "Give Caesar what is his, and give God what is his."

Their mouths hung open, speechless.

¹⁸⁻²³Some Sadducees, the party that denies any possibility of resurrection, came up and asked, "Teacher, Moses wrote that if a man dies and leaves a wife but no child, his brother is obligated to marry the widow and have children. Well, there once were seven brothers. The first took a wife. He died childless. The second married her. He died, and still no child. The same with the third. All seven took their turn, but no child. Finally the wife died. When they are raised at the resurrection, whose wife is she? All seven were her husband."

²⁴⁻²⁷Jesus said, "You're way off base, and here's why: One, you don't know what God said; two, you don't know how God works. After the dead are raised up, we're past the marriage business. As it is with angels now, all our ecstasies and intimacies then will be with God. And regarding the dead, whether or not they are raised, don't you ever read the Bible? How God at the bush said to Moses, 'I am—not *was*—the God of Abraham, the God of Isaac, and the God of Jacob'? The living God is God of the *living*, not the dead. You're way, way off base."

²⁸One of the religion scholars came up. Hearing the lively exchanges of question and answer and seeing how sharp Jesus was in his answers, he put in his question: "Which is most important of all the commandments?"

²⁹⁻³¹Jesus said, "The first in importance is, 'Listen, Israel: The Lord your God is one; so love the Lord God with all your passion and prayer and intelligence and energy.' And here is the second: 'Love others as well as you love yourself.' There is no other commandment that ranks with these."

³²⁻³³The religion scholar said, "A wonderful answer, Teacher! So clear-cut and accurate—that God is one and there is no other. And loving him with all passion and intelligence and energy, and loving others as well as you love yourself. Why, that's better than all offerings and sacrifices put together!"

³⁴When Jesus realized how insightful he was, he said, "You're almost there, right on the border of God's kingdom."

After that, no one else dared ask a question.

After the Passage

Not only do the religious leaders ignore Jesus' warning in the previous parable (Mark 12:1-12), but they also make a plan to trick Jesus into saying something that will upset the crowds and politicians of the day (Mark 12:13). They think if they can get Jesus to say something wrong, then they can turn people against Jesus. The problem with this plan? Jesus is infinitely wise and knowledgeable. Every time they try to trick Him, Jesus gives a perfect and astounding answer to their questions.

Perhaps the most significant answer occurs when someone asks the question "Which is most important of all the commandments?" (Mark 12:28). The ultimate trick question! There are literally hundreds of commandments in the Old Testament—how can Jesus pick one over the others? If He picks one commandment, then He ignores the rest of God's Old Testament law. But rather than pick a specific commandment, Jesus recites a line very familiar to a Jewish person in His time: Deuteronomy 6:4-5, a passage known as the Shema (Mark 12:29-31). It serves as a great reminder to the Jewish people of who God is and what His expectations are for His people. When Jesus references this line as a response to the question, He essentially concludes that the most important law is not actually a law at all—it is the command to love God (Mark 12:29-30). He continues by saying that loving your neighbor is the second greatest commandment (Mark 12:31). With these two instructions, Jesus summarizes the entire law into two simple truths, and everyone listening is amazed (Mark 12:32-34).

The Bottom Line

Love God. Love others.

EXPERIENCE

Every coin has two sides: heads and tails. You cannot have a coin without both sides—a one-sided coin simply does not exist! Jesus' command to love God and love others is like the two sides of the following-God coin. You have to love both to truly follow God.

How can you love God and others today?

HOW I WILL LOVE GOD TODAY	HOW I WILL LOVE OTHERS TODAY

FIND A COIN AND KEEP IT
CLOSE. WHEN YOU SEE IT
OR TOUCH IT, THINK ABOUT
THE HEADS SIDE AS LOVING
GOD AND THE TAILS SIDE
AS LOVING OTHERS.

Takeaway and Pray

My takeaway from this experience is

My prayer today is a

__ REQUEST __ CONFESSION __ PRAISE

a mighty offering

Mark 12:35-44

Know before You Go

Jesus continues to teach at the Temple and challenge the religious leaders' conclusions and values.

Read the Passage

12:35-37While he was teaching in the Temple, Jesus asked, "How is it that the religion scholars say that the Messiah is David's 'son,' when we all know that David, inspired by the Holy Spirit, said,

> God said to my Master,
>   "Sit here at my right hand
>   until I put your enemies under your feet."

"David here designates the Messiah 'my Master'—so how can the Messiah also be his 'son'?"

The large crowd was delighted with what they heard.

³⁸⁻⁴⁰He continued teaching. "Watch out for the religion scholars. They love to walk around in academic gowns, preening in the radiance of public flattery, basking in prominent positions, sitting at the head table at every church function. And all the time they are exploiting the weak and helpless. The longer their prayers, the worse they get. But they'll pay for it in the end."

⁴¹⁻⁴⁴Sitting across from the offering box, he was observing how the crowd tossed money in for the collection. Many of the rich were making large contributions. One poor widow came up and put in two small coins—a measly two cents. Jesus called his disciples over and said, "The truth is that this poor widow gave more to the collection than all the others put together. All the others gave what they'll never miss; she gave extravagantly what she couldn't afford—she gave her all."

After the Passage

The widow's offering in Mark 12:41-44 serves as another example of Jesus' counter-cultural values. The wealthy give significantly more money than the woman (Mark 12:41). To understand their giving in modern-day amounts, the wealthy give around a hundred dollars, and the woman gives twenty-five cents. Despite the large contributions of many wealthy individuals, Jesus proclaims that the incredibly small gift from the widow is the most generous gift of that day (Mark 12:43). In what world is a quarter worth more than a hundred dollars?

In Jesus' world, He is far more concerned with the condition of our hearts than the value of our stuff. Jesus repeatedly reminds His disciples that the first shall be last. While the amount of the widow's offering is quite small, it is everything she has. She selflessly gives her resources to bless others and obey God. Her heart is pure and others focused. The rich selfishly give only a small fraction of their fortune. Their hearts are hard and selfish.

This small scene also reinforces Jesus' instructions to not prioritize the wealth, stuff, and distractions of this world over a relationship with God. The heart of the widow contrasts with the heart of the rich man Jesus meets in Mark 10. That rich man cannot imagine giving up his possessions to have a relationship with God. This widow voluntarily gives all she has out of obedience and love for God!

The Bottom Line

True generosity reflects the condition of our hearts rather than the value of our giving.

EXPERIENCE

Be generous to someone today. It may mean buying someone lunch, it may mean giving away your hard-earned allowance, or it may mean sharing your favorite thing with someone else.

Takeaway and Pray

My takeaway from this experience is

My prayer today is a

__ REQUEST __ CONFESSION __ PRAISE

not when but watch

Mark 13:1-37

Know before You Go

Jesus discusses the end of this world and the coming of His Kingdom.

Read the Passage

¹³:¹As he walked away from the Temple, one of his disciples said, "Teacher, look at that stonework! Those buildings!"

²Jesus said, "You're impressed by this grandiose architecture? There's not a stone in the whole works that is not going to end up in a heap of rubble."

³⁻⁴Later, as he was sitting on Mount Olives in full view of the Temple, Peter, James, John, and Andrew got him off by himself and asked, "Tell us, when is this going to happen? What sign will we get that things are coming to a head?"

⁵⁻⁸Jesus began, "Watch out for doomsday deceivers. Many leaders are going to show up with forged identities claiming, 'I'm the One.' They will deceive a lot of people. When you hear of wars and rumored wars, keep your head and don't panic. This is routine history, and no sign of the end. Nation will fight nation and ruler fight ruler, over and over. Earthquakes will occur in various places. There will be famines. But these things are nothing compared to what's coming.

9-10"And watch out! They're going to drag you into court. And then it will go from bad to worse, dog-eat-dog, everyone at your throat because you carry my name. You're placed there as sentinels to truth. The Message has to be preached all across the world.

11"When they bring you, betrayed, into court, don't worry about what you'll say. When the time comes, say what's on your heart—the Holy Spirit will make his witness in and through you.

12-13"It's going to be brother killing brother, father killing child, children killing parents. There's no telling who will hate you because of me.

"Stay with it—that's what is required. Stay with it to the end. You won't be sorry; you'll be saved.

14-18"But be ready to run for it when you see the monster of desecration set up where it should *never* be. You who can read, make sure you understand what I'm talking about. If you're living in Judea at the time, run for the hills; if you're working in the yard, don't go back to the house to get anything; if you're out in the field, don't go back to get your coat. Pregnant and nursing mothers will have it especially hard. Hope and pray this won't happen in the middle of winter.

19-20"These are going to be hard days—nothing like it from the time God made the world right up to the present. And there'll be nothing like it again. If he let the days of trouble run their course, nobody would make it. But because of God's chosen people, those he personally chose, he has already intervened.

21-23"If anyone tries to flag you down, calling out, 'Here's the Messiah!' or points, 'There he is!' don't fall for it. Fake Messiahs and lying preachers are going to pop up everywhere. Their impressive credentials and bewitching performances will pull the wool over the eyes of even those who ought to know better. So watch out. I've given you fair warning.

24-25"Following those hard times,

Sun will fade out,
    moon cloud over,
Stars fall out of the sky,
    cosmic powers tremble.

²⁶⁻²⁷"And then they'll see the Son of Man enter in grand style, his Arrival filling the sky—no one will miss it! He'll dispatch the angels; they will pull in the chosen from the four winds, from pole to pole.

²⁸⁻³¹"Take a lesson from the fig tree. From the moment you notice its buds form, the merest hint of green, you know summer's just around the corner. And so it is with you. When you see all these things, you know he is at the door. Don't take this lightly. I'm not just saying this for some future generation, but for this one, too—these things will happen. Sky and earth will wear out; my words won't wear out.

³²⁻³⁷"But the exact day and hour? No one knows that, not even heaven's angels, not even the Son. Only the Father. So keep a sharp lookout, for you don't know the timetable. It's like a man who takes a trip, leaving home and putting his servants in charge, each assigned a task, and commanding the gatekeeper to stand watch. So, stay at your post, watching. You have no idea when the homeowner is returning, whether evening, midnight, cockcrow, or morning. You don't want him showing up unannounced, with you asleep on the job. I say it to you, and I'm saying it to all: Stay at your post. Keep watch."

After the Passage

For those interested in the end times, Mark 13 is a jackpot! This chapter includes all sorts of warnings, signs, and end times language. But for most people, the chapter is confusing, is a bit scary, and seemingly lacks any sort of practical applications.

While Jesus' teaching in Mark 13 is certainly fascinating, we sometimes over-complicate this passage by trying to interpret Jesus' words in a way that He doesn't intend us to. For instance, some teachers may try to use these words to help determine exactly what the end of the earth will look like, what will happen, when it will happen, and how it will happen. The problem with this approach is that Jesus does not want us to draw those conclusions from this text.

So if Jesus is not trying to give us an exact end times timeline, what is He trying to do? Do you notice any themes or repeated words in His sermon? Look for phrases like *watch out* and *keep a sharp lookout* (Mark 13:5, 9, 23, 33-37). It seems that Jesus is trying to appeal to our hearts rather than teach end times theology. He warns us to stay pure, avoid temptation, and be aware that He can come back at any time. We need to avoid the pressure of this world and not compromise what we believe about God.

Hundreds of generations have come and gone without Jesus returning or the world ending. The question we need to ask ourselves is *Am I ready for Jesus to come back?* and not *Will Jesus come back in my lifetime?* We need to stand firm in our faith in Jesus and watch out for things that can turn us away from Him.

The Bottom Line

We should be ready for Jesus to return at any time.

EXPERIENCE

This passage is not meant to scare us or help us predict the timing of Jesus' return. Instead, this passage should urge us to live our lives as if Jesus is coming back tomorrow!

WHAT IS ONE
CHANGE YOU WOULD
WANT TO MAKE IN
YOUR LIFE TODAY IF
YOU KNEW JESUS
WAS COMING BACK
TOMORROW?

Takeaway and Pray

My takeaway from this experience is

My prayer today is a

__ REQUEST __ CONFESSION __ PRAISE

your choice

Mark 14:1-26

Know before You Go

Jesus interacts with a poor woman who selflessly serves Him. Then He shares the Last Supper with His disciples, predicts His betrayal, and offers the first Communion.

Read the Passage

14:1-2In only two days the eight-day Festival of Passover and the Feast of Unleavened Bread would begin. The high priests and religion scholars were looking for a way they could seize Jesus by stealth and kill him. They agreed that it should not be done during Passover Week. "We don't want the crowds up in arms," they said.

3-5Jesus was at Bethany, a guest of Simon the Leper. While he was eating dinner, a woman came up carrying a bottle of very expensive perfume. Opening the bottle, she poured it on his head. Some of the guests became furious among themselves. "That's criminal! A sheer waste! This perfume could have been sold for well over a year's wages and handed out to the poor." They swelled up in anger, nearly bursting with indignation over her.

⁶⁻⁹But Jesus said, "Let her alone. Why are you giving her a hard time? She has just done something wonderfully significant for me. You will have the poor with you every day for the rest of your lives. Whenever you feel like it, you can do something for them. Not so with me. She did what she could when she could—she pre-anointed my body for burial. And you can be sure that wherever in the whole world the Message is preached, what she just did is going to be talked about admiringly."

¹⁰⁻¹¹Judas Iscariot, one of the Twelve, went to the cabal of high priests, determined to betray him. They couldn't believe their ears, and promised to pay him well. He started looking for just the right moment to hand him over.

¹²On the first of the Days of Unleavened Bread, the day they prepare the Passover sacrifice, his disciples asked him, "Where do you want us to go and make preparations so you can eat the Passover meal?"

¹³⁻¹⁵He directed two of his disciples, "Go into the city. A man carrying a water jug will meet you. Follow him. Ask the owner of whichever house he enters, 'The Teacher wants to know, Where is my guest room where I can eat the Passover meal with my disciples?' He will show you a spacious second-story room, swept and ready. Prepare for us there."

¹⁶The disciples left, came to the city, found everything just as he had told them, and prepared the Passover meal.

¹⁷⁻¹⁸After sunset he came with the Twelve. As they were at the supper table eating, Jesus said, "I have something hard but important to say to you: One of you is going to hand me over to the conspirators, one who at this moment is eating with me."

¹⁹Stunned, they started asking, one after another, "It isn't me, is it?"

²⁰⁻²¹He said, "It's one of the Twelve, one who eats with me out of the same bowl. In one sense, it turns out that the Son of Man is entering into a way of treachery well-marked by the Scriptures—no surprises here. In another sense, the man who turns him in, turns traitor to the Son of Man—better never to have been born than do this!"

²²In the course of their meal, having taken and blessed the bread, he broke it and gave it to them. Then he said,

Take, this is my body.

²³⁻²⁴Taking the chalice, he gave it to them, thanking God, and they all drank from it. He said,

This is my blood,
God's new covenant,
Poured out for many people.

²⁵"I'll not be drinking wine again until the new day when I drink it in the kingdom of God."
²⁶They sang a hymn and then went directly to Mount Olives.

After the Passage

In Jesus' final meal with His disciples, He shares some disturbing news: One of His disciples is going to betray Him (Mark 14:18). Look carefully at how the disciples respond to this sad revelation. They do not question Jesus, they do not mourn the news, and they do not ask how they can help stop the betrayal. The disciples' first reaction is to worry! They each ask Jesus if they will be the one to betray Him (Mark 14:19)!

This reaction shows the insecurity, and perhaps the doubt, that the disciples still have about following Jesus. Even after years of hearing His teachings and witnessing His miracles, there still seems to be a hint of nervousness about whether or not they are fully committed to following Jesus.

Your commitment to Jesus must be a personal choice. Judas, the disciple that ultimately betrays Jesus, is further proof that being around the right group of people does not guarantee a personal relationship with Jesus. Christian friends, parents, and teachers are certainly encouraging and beneficial, but each person is responsible for making independent choices. While the other disciples have their moments of doubt, their personal beliefs and convictions allow them to stay faithful to Jesus. The meal Jesus shares with His disciples in Mark 14:22-25 is the spiritual practice of Communion that we can still exercise today. It helps remind us to choose Jesus and reflect on His sacrifice for us.

The Bottom Line

Your choice to follow Jesus must be a personal decision that affects every part of your life.

EXPERIENCE

When are you tempted to hide your faith in God?

When is it easier to pretend that you do not know God or care about what the Bible says?

Write out a prayer to God asking Him to give you the strength to choose Him each day.

ASK GOD FOR THE STRENGTH NOT TO DENY HIM AND NOT TO RELY ON YOURSELF IN DIFFICULT SITUATIONS.

Takeaway and Pray

My takeaway from this experience is

My prayer today is a

__ REQUEST __ CONFESSION __ PRAISE

no greater love

Mark 14:27-72

Know before You Go

This passage begins the story of Jesus' death. First, Jesus predicts that His disciple Peter will deny Him, which Peter does—several times—later. Jesus is also arrested in Gethsemane and put on trial.

Read the Passage

14:27-28 Jesus told them, "You're all going to feel that your world is falling apart and that it's my fault. There's a Scripture that says,

I will strike the shepherd;
The sheep will scatter.

"But after I am raised up, I will go ahead of you, leading the way to Galilee."

29 Peter blurted out, "Even if everyone else is ashamed of you when things fall to pieces, I won't be."

30 Jesus said, "Don't be so sure. Today, this very night in fact, before the rooster crows twice, you will deny me three times."

[31]He blustered in protest, "Even if I have to die with you, I will never deny you." All the others said the same thing.

[32-34]They came to an area called Gethsemane. Jesus told his disciples, "Sit here while I pray." He took Peter, James, and John with him. He sank into a pit of suffocating darkness. He told them, "I feel bad enough right now to die. Stay here and keep vigil with me."

[35-36]Going a little ahead, he fell to the ground and prayed for a way out: "Papa, Father, you can—can't you?—get me out of this. Take this cup away from me. But please, not what I want—what do *you* want?"

[37-38]He came back and found them sound asleep. He said to Peter, "Simon, you went to sleep on me? Can't you stick it out with me a single hour? Stay alert, be in prayer, so you don't enter the danger zone without even knowing it. Don't be naive. Part of you is eager, ready for anything in God; but another part is as lazy as an old dog sleeping by the fire."

[39-40]He then went back and prayed the same prayer. Returning, he again found them sound asleep. They simply couldn't keep their eyes open, and they didn't have a plausible excuse.

[41-42]He came back a third time and said, "Are you going to sleep all night? No— you've slept long enough. Time's up. The Son of Man is about to be betrayed into the hands of sinners. Get up. Let's get going. My betrayer has arrived."

[43-47]No sooner were the words out of his mouth when Judas, the one out of the Twelve, showed up, and with him a bunch of thugs, sent by the high priests, religion scholars, and leaders, brandishing swords and clubs. The betrayer had worked out a signal with them: "The one I kiss, that's the one—seize him. Make sure he doesn't get away." He went straight to Jesus and said, "Rabbi!" and kissed him. The others then grabbed him and roughed him up. One of the men standing there unsheathed his sword, swung, and came down on the Chief Priest's servant, lopping off the man's ear.

[48-50]Jesus said to them, "What is this, coming after me with swords and clubs as if I were a dangerous criminal? Day after day I've been sitting in the Temple teaching, and you never so much as lifted a hand against me. What you in fact have done is confirm the prophetic writings." All the disciples bailed on him.

⁵¹⁻⁵²A young man was following along. All he had on was a bedsheet. Some of the men grabbed him but he got away, running off naked, leaving them holding the sheet.

⁵³⁻⁵⁴They led Jesus to the Chief Priest, where the high priests, religious leaders, and scholars had gathered together. Peter followed at a safe distance until they got to the Chief Priest's courtyard, where he mingled with the servants and warmed himself at the fire.

⁵⁵⁻⁵⁹The high priests conspiring with the Jewish Council looked high and low for evidence against Jesus by which they could sentence him to death. They found nothing. Plenty of people were willing to bring in false charges, but nothing added up, and they ended up canceling each other out. Then a few of them stood up and lied: "We heard him say, 'I am going to tear down this Temple, built by hard labor, and in three days build another without lifting a hand.'" But even they couldn't agree exactly.

⁶⁰⁻⁶¹In the middle of this, the Chief Priest stood up and asked Jesus, "What do you have to say to the accusation?" Jesus was silent. He said nothing.

The Chief Priest tried again, this time asking, "Are you the Messiah, the Son of the Blessed?"

⁶²Jesus said, "Yes, I am, and you'll see it yourself:

The Son of Man seated
At the right hand of the Mighty One,
Arriving on the clouds of heaven."

⁶³⁻⁶⁴The Chief Priest lost his temper. Ripping his clothes, he yelled, "Did you hear that? After that do we need witnesses? You heard the blasphemy. Are you going to stand for it?"

They condemned him, one and all. The sentence: death.

⁶⁵Some of them started spitting at him. They blindfolded his eyes, then hit him, saying, "Who hit you? Prophesy!" The guards, punching and slapping, took him away.

⁶⁶⁻⁶⁷While all this was going on, Peter was down in the courtyard. One of the Chief Priest's servant girls came in and, seeing Peter warming himself there, looked hard at him and said, "You were with the Nazarene, Jesus."

⁶⁸He denied it: "I don't know what you're talking about." He went out on the porch. A rooster crowed.

⁶⁹⁻⁷⁰The girl spotted him and began telling the people standing around, "He's one of them." He denied it again.

After a little while, the bystanders brought it up again. "You've *got* to be one of them. You've got 'Galilean' written all over you."

⁷¹⁻⁷²Now Peter got really nervous and swore, "I never laid eyes on this man you're talking about." Just then the rooster crowed a second time. Peter remembered how Jesus had said, "Before a rooster crows twice, you'll deny me three times." He collapsed in tears.

After the Passage

Jesus' prayer in the garden of Gethsemane shows the depth of His pain and sorrow (Mark 14:32-36). In most of Jesus' interactions, we see that He is God—He performs miracles and teaches with amazing authority. In this scene, however, we see that Jesus is also fully human. Like any other human, Jesus is hurting and feels deep sorrow for what is to come. He is fully aware of the awful things that await Him in the next few days, and it is His deep desire to avoid them if at all possible. Amazingly enough, Jesus prays that He will do whatever God wants! Even in His pain and sorrow, Jesus provides an amazing example of someone who trusts in God's plan no matter the cost.

After His arrest in Gethsemane, Jesus is brought before a Jewish court (Mark 14:53-65). Even after His arrest and trial, the religious leaders are unable to prove Jesus has done anything wrong! Finally, when they directly ask Jesus if He is the Son of God, He replies truthfully, "I am" (Mark 14:61-62). If someone falsely claims to be the Son of God, the Jewish people have the right to punish this person. However, Jesus *is* the Son of God. Nevertheless, the court does not believe His claim and finds Jesus guilty of lying! In Mark 14:66-72, Peter also fails to recognize Jesus' true identity. Even though Peter believes Jesus to be the Son of God, his current fear and worry causes him to deny his Savior.

As we learn from these interactions in Mark 14, what we believe about Jesus is incredibly important! Do you believe He is God? Do you trust Him no matter what? Do you think He is a liar pretending to be God's Son? Do you doubt Him in times of stress?

The Bottom Line

Jesus loves us despite our reactions to Him.

EXPERIENCE

For an entire day, keep track of how many times you hear the word *love*.

What are some things we typically say we love?

How is the love that Jesus displays for us different from other types of love?

What is your response to Jesus' love?

Takeaway and Pray

My takeaway from this experience is

My prayer today is a

__ REQUEST __ CONFESSION __ PRAISE

amazing grace

Mark 15:1-20

Know before You Go

The religious leaders turn to someone with the authority to sentence Jesus to death. The Roman leader, Pilate, transfers the status of a criminal, Barabbas, onto Jesus.

Read the Passage

15:1At dawn's first light, the high priests, with the religious leaders and scholars, arranged a conference with the entire Jewish Council. After tying Jesus securely, they took him out and presented him to Pilate.

2-3Pilate asked him, "Are you the 'King of the Jews'?"

He answered, "If you say so." The high priests let loose a barrage of accusations.

4-5Pilate asked again, "Aren't you going to answer anything? That's quite a list of accusations." Still, he said nothing. Pilate was impressed, really impressed.

6-10It was a custom at the Feast to release a prisoner, anyone the people asked for. There was one prisoner called Barabbas, locked up with the insurrectionists who had committed murder during the uprising against Rome. As the crowd came up and began to present its petition for him to release a prisoner, Pilate anticipated them: "Do you want me to release the King of the Jews to you?" Pilate knew by this time that it was through sheer spite that the high priests had turned Jesus over to him.

¹¹⁻¹²But the high priests by then had worked up the crowd to ask for the release of Barabbas. Pilate came back, "So what do I do with this man you call King of the Jews?"

¹³They yelled, "Nail him to a cross!"

¹⁴Pilate objected, "But for what crime?"

But they yelled all the louder, "Nail him to a cross!"

¹⁵Pilate gave the crowd what it wanted, set Barabbas free and turned Jesus over for whipping and crucifixion.

¹⁶⁻²⁰The soldiers took Jesus into the palace (called Praetorium) and called together the entire brigade. They dressed him up in purple and put a crown plaited from a thornbush on his head. Then they began their mockery: "Bravo, King of the Jews!" They banged on his head with a club, spit on him, and knelt down in mock worship. After they had had their fun, they took off the purple cape and put his own clothes back on him. Then they marched out to nail him to the cross.

After the Passage

After Jesus' appearance before the Jewish court, He goes before the Roman government and meets a man named Pilate (Mark 15:1). Pilate experiences the same problem the religious leaders experienced in court the night before: Pilate is unable to find Jesus guilty.

Although Pilate knows Jesus is innocent, he lets fear direct his decision. Pilate fears what the crowd will think of him if he does not hand Jesus over to be crucified. The people want Jesus dead (Mark 15:10-15), and the politician in Pilate cares more about his position of power than protecting the truth. Pilate chooses to release a man named Barabbas, a convicted criminal who actually deserves to be in jail, and lets the religious leaders continue their plan to kill Jesus (Mark 15:15).

While this decision to transfer Barabbas's punishment onto Jesus is incredibly unfair, it is a picture of why Jesus came to earth: to set the prisoner free and forgive the guilty. Barabbas does not deserve to be set free; he should pay the penalty for his sins. Yet, because Jesus takes his place as a prisoner, Barabbas is able to have a new life. We, too, are guilty of doing wrong and sinning. We, too, are lost without Jesus.

And we, too, can be set free and have a new life because of Jesus' perfect sacrifice! In some ways, Barabbas is the first to experience the grace of the Cross!

The Bottom Line

Jesus saves us from the punishment we deserve by taking it upon Himself.

EXPERIENCE

Think of a time you gave grace to a person who did not deserve it. What was it?

Think of a time you received grace you did not deserve. What was it?

How did you feel during both of these interactions?

SPEND A FEW MINUTES THANKING JESUS FOR GIVING YOU GRACE YOU DO NOT DESERVE.

Takeaway and Pray

My takeaway from this experience is

My prayer today is a

__ REQUEST __ CONFESSION __ PRAISE

life through death

Mark 15:21-47

Know before You Go

This passage describes the pain and suffering Jesus experiences during His crucifixion. Jesus' body is then buried in a tomb nearby.

Read the Passage

15:21There was a man walking by, coming from work, Simon from Cyrene, the father of Alexander and Rufus. They made him carry Jesus' cross.

22-24The soldiers brought Jesus to Golgotha, meaning "Skull Hill." They offered him a mild painkiller (wine mixed with myrrh), but he wouldn't take it. And they nailed him to the cross. They divided up his clothes and threw dice to see who would get them.

25-30They nailed him up at nine o'clock in the morning. The charge against him— THE KING OF THE JEWS—was scrawled across a sign. Along with him, they crucified two criminals, one to his right, the other to his left. People passing along the road jeered, shaking their heads in mock lament: "You bragged that you could tear down the Temple and then rebuild it in three days—so show us your stuff! Save yourself! If you're really God's Son, come down from that cross!"

³¹⁻³²The high priests, along with the religion scholars, were right there mixing it up with the rest of them, having a great time poking fun at him: "He saved others—but he can't save himself! Messiah, is he? King of Israel? Then let him climb down from that cross. We'll *all* become believers then!" Even the men crucified alongside him joined in the mockery.

³³⁻³⁴At noon the sky became extremely dark. The darkness lasted three hours. At three o'clock, Jesus groaned out of the depths, crying loudly, "*Eloi, Eloi, lama sabachthani?*" which means, "My God, my God, why have you abandoned me?"

³⁵⁻³⁶Some of the bystanders who heard him said, "Listen, he's calling for Elijah." Someone ran off, soaked a sponge in sour wine, put it on a stick, and gave it to him to drink, saying, "Let's see if Elijah comes to take him down."

³⁷⁻³⁹But Jesus, with a loud cry, gave his last breath. At that moment the Temple curtain ripped right down the middle. When the Roman captain standing guard in front of him saw that he had quit breathing, he said, "This has to be the Son of God!"

⁴⁰⁻⁴¹There were women watching from a distance, among them Mary Magdalene, Mary the mother of the younger James and Joses, and Salome. When Jesus was in Galilee, these women followed and served him, and had come up with him to Jerusalem.

⁴²⁻⁴⁵Late in the afternoon, since it was the Day of Preparation (that is, Sabbath eve), Joseph of Arimathea, a highly respected member of the Jewish Council, came. He was one who lived expectantly, on the lookout for the kingdom of God. Working up his courage, he went to Pilate and asked for Jesus' body. Pilate questioned whether he could be dead that soon and called for the captain to verify that he was really dead. Assured by the captain, he gave Joseph the corpse.

⁴⁶⁻⁴⁷Having already purchased a linen shroud, Joseph took him down, wrapped him in the shroud, placed him in a tomb that had been cut into the rock, and rolled a large stone across the opening. Mary Magdalene and Mary, mother of Joses, watched the burial.

After the Passage

Over the past couple of chapters of Mark, you read about the brutal torture Jesus endured in the final days of His life. The beatings, insults, and mockery ultimately lead to death by crucifixion. Crucifixion is an incredibly painful and humiliating way to die. It is a punishment reserved for the worst of the worst because of its severity. Why does Jesus have to die this way?

Simply put, Jesus' crucifixion shows us the severity of our sin, the extent of Jesus' humility, and the depth of His love for us. If Jesus is to pay the ultimate price for our sins, He needs to actually pay the price. The punishment for a criminal is to be whipped, beaten, and killed. Even though Jesus has never sinned and is perfectly holy, He takes on the punishment completely. Jesus' crucifixion serves as the ultimate example of humility and love.

Finally, it proves how much God loves us. Jesus endures such suffering to have a relationship with us. When Jesus finally dies, an incredible miracle happens in the Temple (Mark 15:37-39). There is a large curtain that divides the common places of the Temple from the Holy of Holies, a space where God's Spirit dwells. Only the high priest can enter the Holy of Holies, and the curtain serves as a stopping point for everyone else. In Mark 15:38, God tears the curtain in half from top to bottom. This tear is incredibly symbolic—everyone can now interact with God. We are not limited or restricted, we are free from sin, and we are free to experience a relationship with God through Jesus' death on the cross!

The Bottom Line

While brutal to read about, the Crucifixion is how we can understand Jesus' mission, His love for us, and the gift of salvation!

EXPERIENCE

The cross has been a symbol of Christianity for two thousand years. For some people, the cross is just a nice piece of jewelry or an interesting thing to put on a wall. For others, the cross is a great reminder of how much Jesus loves them. How many crosses do you see in an average week? (It would be interesting to actually keep track!)

The cross is a reminder that Jesus loves you. When you see a cross, think of Jesus literally saying "I love you." When you see a cross, pray the words *I love You too* back to Jesus to continually remind yourself of the love displayed by the Cross.

† = I LOVE YOU

Takeaway and Pray

My takeaway from this experience is

My prayer today is a

__ REQUEST __ CONFESSION __ PRAISE

risen, indeed!

Mark 16:1-8

Know before You Go

Three days later, Mary Magdalene discovers that Jesus' tomb is empty. Jesus has risen from the dead and is alive!

Read the Passage

16:1-3When the Sabbath was over, Mary Magdalene, Mary the mother of James, and Salome bought spices so they could embalm him. Very early on Sunday morning, as the sun rose, they went to the tomb. They worried out loud to each other, "Who will roll back the stone from the tomb for us?"

4-5Then they looked up, saw that it had been rolled back—it was a huge stone—and walked right in. They saw a young man sitting on the right side, dressed all in white. They were completely taken aback, astonished.

6-7He said, "Don't be afraid. I know you're looking for Jesus the Nazarene, the One they nailed on the cross. He's been raised up; he's here no longer. You can see for yourselves that the place is empty. Now—on your way. Tell his disciples and

Peter that he is going on ahead of you to Galilee. You'll see him there, exactly as he said."

⁸They got out as fast as they could, beside themselves, their heads swimming. Stunned, they said nothing to anyone.

After the Passage

The hours following Jesus' death have to be some of the most confusing and depressing hours in all human history. For those following Jesus and believing Him to be the Son of God, His death must shatter their hopes and expectations. As we learn in Mark 11, the people think Jesus is going to save them from their current Roman rulers. Now it seems as though they have placed their hope in the wrong person. It seems as though the religious leaders who have opposed Jesus are in fact correct: Jesus' death must mean that He is a fraud, because the Son of God should not die. Jesus' disciples must be asking themselves, *Should we still follow Jesus' teachings or go back to believing the Pharisees?*

It is hard to imagine the sadness, frustration, and disappointment that those closest to Jesus must feel when Jesus dies because we know the ending—we know that Jesus does not stay dead! The fact that Jesus rises from the dead validates everything He says He is! His resurrection is the ultimate proof that He is the Son of God. The women's fearful reaction in Mark 16:8 is incredibly understandable—Jesus has conquered death! Amazing!

For a follower of Jesus, there are no sweeter words than "He's been raised up; he's here no longer" (Mark 16:6). It is the resurrection of Jesus that gives us hope. It is the reason we can have confidence in our faith. It is why we can read a Gospel (like Mark) and try our best to put Jesus' words into practice. Jesus' resurrection proves that His teachings are true and worth following!

The Bottom Line

Jesus is alive and is the Savior of the world!

EXPERIENCE

What are some of your doubts about God?

Sometimes doubting can force us to ask healthy questions about our faith. Who in your life can help you process some of these questions or doubts?

Is Jesus the Savior of your life? Write a prayer that reflects the answer to this question.

Takeaway and Pray

My takeaway from this experience is

My prayer today is a

__ REQUEST __ CONFESSION __ PRAISE

go & tell!

Mark 16:9-20

Know before You Go

It's hard to tell exactly where these verses come from—the original author (Mark) or authors later in the process. Mark 16:9-20 is not found in the earliest handwritten copies. Nevertheless, we can still learn from these verses because they include Jesus' instructions to His disciples before He returns to heaven.

Read the Passage

¹⁶:⁹⁻¹¹[After rising from the dead, Jesus appeared early on Sunday morning to Mary Magdalene, whom he had delivered from seven demons. She went to his former companions, now weeping and carrying on, and told them. When they heard her report that she had seen him alive and well, they didn't believe her.

¹²⁻¹³Later he appeared, but in a different form, to two of them out walking in the countryside. They went back and told the rest, but they weren't believed either.

¹⁴⁻¹⁶Still later, as the Eleven were eating supper, he appeared and took them to task most severely for their stubborn unbelief, refusing to believe those who had seen him raised up. Then he said, "Go into the world. Go everywhere and announce

the Message of God's good news to one and all. Whoever believes and is baptized is saved; whoever refuses to believe is damned.

[17-18]"These are some of the signs that will accompany believers: They will throw out demons in my name, they will speak in new tongues, they will take snakes in their hands, they will drink poison and not be hurt, they will lay hands on the sick and make them well."

[19-20]Then the Master Jesus, after briefing them, was taken up to heaven, and he sat down beside God in the place of honor. And the disciples went everywhere preaching, the Master working right with them, validating the Message with indisputable evidence.]

Note: Mark 16:9-20 [the portion in brackets] is not found in the earliest handwritten copies.

After the Passage

At the end of the Gospel of Mark, Jesus shows Himself to be the Son of God. He meets with Mary and the disciples, and He restores their faith in Him (Mark 16:9-14).

In His final moments on earth, Jesus instructs the disciples to spread His message and teachings to the far corners of the earth (Mark 16:15). And they do (Mark 16:20)! Through the power of God, they change the future of the world in Jesus' name. The fact that we are still talking about Jesus all over the world today is evidence of the disciples' obedience to Jesus' instructions!

We have come to the end of the Gospel of Mark. The teachings of Jesus recorded in this Gospel are not just stories; they are the actual events of the earthly life of God's Son. The message is true and directly from the mouth of God. This Gospel shows us a better way to live. This Gospel turns our world upside down and sets our priorities on spiritual things rather than physical things. Remember, you must personally answer the question *Who is Jesus?* Your answer is the most important thing in your life.

The Bottom Line

Tell everyone you meet about Jesus and what He means to you!

EXPERIENCE

Take a moment to reflect on your accomplishment. You have now read the entire Gospel of Mark!

Write down something you learned, a way you'll think of Jesus differently, and a way you'll change your behavior now that you've read the Gospel of Mark.

SOMETHING I LEARNED	HOW I WILL THINK DIFFERENTLY ABOUT JESUS	HOW I WILL ACT DIFFERENTLY

Takeaway and Pray

My takeaway from this experience is

My prayer today is a

__ REQUEST __ CONFESSION __ PRAISE

EXPERIENCE SCRIPTURE

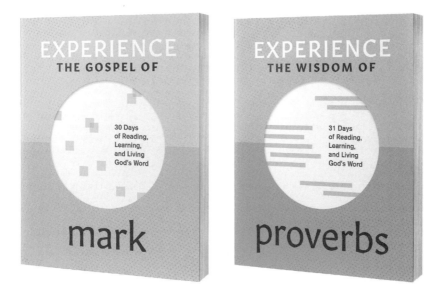

EXPERIENCE
THE GOSPEL OF

30 Days
of Reading,
Learning,
and Living
God's Word

mark

EXPERIENCE
THE WISDOM OF

31 Days
of Reading,
Learning,
and Living
God's Word

proverbs

The Bible is meant to be experienced.
Follow Jesus and the storyline of Scripture
for one month, and see how much your life
will change. Both studies are rooted in
Scripture, accessible, and experiential.

CP1964

THE MESSAGE STUDENT BIBLE

Understand and enjoy the wisdom and beauty of God's Word! Generation after generation of Bible readers have discovered that the Bible is written not only about us but also to us. In these pages we become insiders in a conversation in which God forms, guides, and ultimately saves us.

THE MESSAGE FOR GRADUATES

Encounter biblical direction and encouragement for graduates. There are transition points in every life. Graduation is such a transition point: It marks the end of one life stage and the beginning of another. The demands on your life, the complexity of your challenges, the things that bring you joy, and the things that cause you stress—they're different once you've moved from student life to this new season. This book helps you through that transition.

Find these and other great Bibles and Bible resources at messagebible.com.

CP1965